Self-expansion

psychology simplified

STUDENT EDITION

by Miklós Fodor

Psychology 2.0 Books, Budapest
www.psychology2.org
miklos.fodor@psy2.org
2009

CONTENTS

1. INTRODUCTION TO THE MAIN CONCEPT (FIPP)

Defining the FIPP's basic terms: Self, Environment and cognitive schemata. * The FIPP-pattern: Self-narrowing and Self-expansion. * Converting Self-narrowing into Self-expansion with a new cognitive schema. * Spreading the word of that new schema. * Self-confidence * The competitive evolutionary edge of happiness.

In this introduction, I present an overview of the model used throughout this book. The model examines what roles happiness or communication play in the humans' ability to adapt. An alternative approach to this question is: from an evolutionary perspective, what created the various states of mind, and why do we communicate with others at all? This seemingly too abstract, philosophical question is closely related to the concept that relates most to human existence, namely, the Self. (Henceforth, the redefined concepts of Self and Environment are indicated with an upper-case initial). The Self – one's ability to reflect on one's own existence – has a key role in the appearance of communication and emotions. By clarifying the motivation underlying these basic human characteristics, I believe that I can provide an explanation for various types of behavior, reactions, and social phenomena.

What is self-confidence?

The notion of Self cannot be avoided in psychology: it surfaces in psychoanalysis, cognitive sciences, and social psychology. It is nevertheless less widely used in an everyday sense. Instead, people tend to use a similar notion, namely, self-confidence. Moreover, self-confidence is a key concept in today's success-driven society, which, for many people, is a precondition for good performance or a happy life. This is no mere coincidence. Self-confidence is none other than the relative size of the Self.

What do I mean by this? Probably everyone knows, or has met, a person who has far more self-confidence than the average person. In some, we may feel that the person is rightly proud of themselves. In others, however, there may be no real reason for this.Some people may excel in some area or other, or are proud of a certain skill or capability. Nevertheless, we maynot necessarily notice these people due to their lack of confidence, or they simply may not find it easy to get along in life. Perhaps the most interesting phenomenon is when self-confidence changes: a reticent person suddenly becomes verbose and overtly self-confident, or someone who has always stood up for themselves becomes anxious and uncertain.

A consequence that can be deduced in the latter case is of self-confidence not being a permanent property, such as height, but changeable. If we observe our-selves, we can notice changes in our self-confidence within a single day. Therefore, does our Self, using the size of which we have defined self-confidence, undergo change?

To answer this question, we need firstly to understand what the Self is composed of. There are many definitions of Self in psychological literature. I recommend adhering to a simple definition, namely: let us take the Self as a camera, through the viewfinder of which it is possible to perceive events taking place in the outside world, and which is capable of inducing changes in the surrounding world. What the camera 'sees' at a given moment is what we will call "Environment" (with a capital E to distinguish it from environment used in the general sense, such as nature). The camera, the Self, decides how to react to the basis of incoming information, for which it is equipped with devices capable of processing this incoming information. These devices are what we call cognitive schemata*[1], which term refers to the way thinking (cognition) is comprised of units. These schemata build on one another (as we will see later) to form, amongst other things, categories or words and sentences.

How does self-confidence relate to what the camera sees? Everything is fine if we are simply admiring through a camera's viewfinder a calm, grassy plain. However, if we notice a lion in the distance, we become less confident, and may lose our self-confidence when the camera focuses on the lion and we see that the animal has noticed us. Therefore, the wider and more detailed we see the Environment, the less we will be aware of the camera i.e. our Self. This Self-Environment relationship is, in general terms, labeled self-confidence.

The way we feel is what truly counts: is it the Environment that is controlling us, or do we control the Environment? If we experience that our Self is big, the reason for this is that we feel, at least in the given situation, that we can achieve anything. If we feel tiny, we feel helpless; that the Environment may destroy us at any given moment, or at least cause serious damage.

What have cognitive schemata to do with this? How large we experience our Environment depends upon whether we have any schemata with the help of which we are able to control the Environment. A schema generally implies an understanding of something i.e. having a certain sort of knowledge. It attempts to map the structure and logic of the Environment to a degree that not only enables us to understand how the Environment functions, but effectively influence the way it functions through this knowledge. This creates a feeling of power i.e. it makes us feel self-confident.

We have reached the point of explaining happiness, since self-confidence and the feeling of power is also a positive emotion; it makes us feel happy and joyful.

---

[1]   definitions of the terms marked * also appear in the glossary.

What is the competitive evolutionary edge of happiness?

We have seen that happiness appears if we manage to gain control over the parts of the Environment that are important to us. But why do we need to feel anything at all? If we were not to feel anything when we control the Environment (the sensation of Self-expansion, or happiness in the general sense), nor when we are subject to the whims of the Environment (the sensation of Self-narrowing or anxiety), we would simply not do anything at all. We would not move, and would be under-motivated. Without movement, reaction and adaptation, we would quickly be destroyed; say, as if a lion approaches, and we take no notice of it. There is nothing wrong with this on its own accord; nature would still work perfectly without our adaptation. However, the way evolution works is that anyone who fails to adapt will, generally, not multiply either; this species, therefore, sooner or later become extinct. Therefore, the fact that we are living here and now demonstrates that human beings are a species whose ancestors were equipped with a certain property. Namely, a feedback circle that tells us

Figure 1: Self-expansion and Self-narowing

both that it is worthwhile adapting and that it is hazardous to be at the mercy of the Environment. Today, there are no descendants of those who were not equipped with this.

What exactly is this adaptation that is capable of expanding the Self to such an extent? Cognitive schemata function like models: they grasp certain main aspects of what we experience as the Environment. Some schemata manage to do this well, whilst others do not. Schemata that fail to adequately grasp the key components of the Environment will, sooner or later, end up in contradiction either with a given property of the Environment or of another schema. To take a different approach: the way we know that our schemata are dysfunctional is that they sometimes generate the same response, whilst in other cases they generate a different response to the same Environment as another of our schemata. Whenever we experience our schemata as dysfunctional, we set these schemata aside (in other words, suspend their use) and put all our energy into fathoming this schema so as to make it a well-functioning one.

How, then, can we turn a dysfunctional schema into one that functions well? A watch repairer takes apart a watch that does not work properly, replaces the broken part, and then puts it back together (rebuilds it). So we too take our schemata to pieces (which, as we know, is also composed of schemata) and then put it back together in a different way, to see whether it will produce more adequate or appropriate responses like this. If it does not, we disassemble it again – and again – until it begins to generate responses adjusted to our needs. If two schemata are antagonistic, we need to disassemble both schemata and attempt to create a common schema that dissolves this antagonism (schemata integration); this common schema will be equipped with the same knowledge as that of the two separate schemata.

Since we take the Self as the totality of our schemata, whenever we excise a given schema or a group of schemata because we feel they are faulty, the size of the Self shrinks. This is like a clock that haphazardly stops from time to time. When it is taken to be repaired, we miss the clock even if it functioned properly only occasionally. This demonstrates that, in many cases, a lot of things need to go wrong before things get better (we have to do without the clock while it is away for repair). Another example that shows a temporary decrease in performance while restructuring something: in order to make our room more comfortable, we need first to disorder it by moving the furniture. This may make it difficult even to find a place to sit, apart from the temporary inability to use the room.

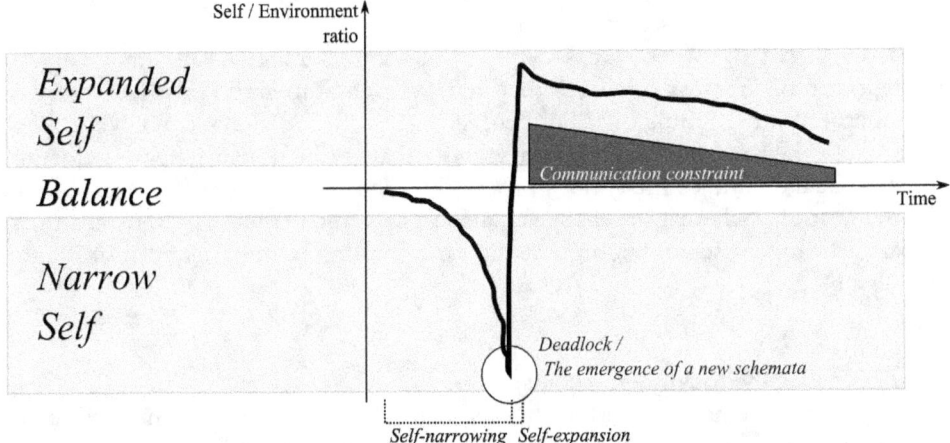

Figure 2: The FIPP-pattern

A newly-repaired schema generally connects better to other schemata than does its predecessor. This implies that the size of our Self has also increased (in absolute value) in relation to the beginning of the process, although it may have reached its nadir midway through. This point the nadir (or deadlock, to use a different term) is when all of the schemata required to put a well-functioning schema together have already been disassembled, and for this reason our Self is at its smallest size during the course of this process (FIPP-pattern).

Why do we communicate?

There are reasons as to why people communicate, such as the need to cooperate. Knowledge transfer is another relevant function. When we imagine a happy person, we rarely imagine them as sitting quietly and on their own. Communication is an integral part of happiness, or, as will be seen later, happiness always accompanies an imperative to communicate, and an attraction to companions.

I will again propose arguments similar to those in connection with the competitive evolutionary edge of happiness. Thousands of years ago, there may have been people that might have realized 'something' and felt happy; however, they did not share this knowledge, or anything else, with others. Perhaps another group of people soon defeated this group, simply due they shared their knowledge, which led to the proliferation of immediate knowledge sharing. In this 'winning' group, individuals did not have to discover everything on their own, which is why their group knowledge accumulated. Therefore, the descendants of people that kept ideas to themselves died out, as did those unmotivated to adapt.

A new schema also requires communication from another aspect. An individual begins to use this schema when completely convinced that the schema does function well. When a person takes a clock home from the repair shop, they will check it from time to time to see whether it is still ticking, or by comparing the time it shows with that of other clocks. Similarly, alone, an individual is limited in his ability to test his new (or newly restructured) schema. Rather, it is also necessary to use schemata in the minds of other people. The given individual is unable to confidently use their new schema until they know that it functions well. Consequently, the individual continues the control process by exchanging schemata; which we call communication. Schemata exchanges can be performed using different channels: verbally (through discussions, arguments), or in writing (writing letters, publishing, writing a blog).

To summarize:
- o The Self is the totality of schemata
- o Cognitive schemata convert information from the Environment into action
- o The quality of cognitive schemata determines whether the Environment or the Self is bigger
- o If the Environment is bigger, we experience Self-narrowing
- o If the Self is bigger, we experience Self-expansion
- o Control over the Environment may be realized with the help of a new schema
- o In most cases, several schemata need to fall to pieces for a new schema to be created; the various parts connect to form a new schema
- o The new, well-functioning schema engenders Self-expansion
- o The new schema needs to be tested; it has to be connected to other schemata
- o Once schemata inside the individual has been compared (tested), it then needs to be compared with the schemata of other persons
- o Schemata testing with others engenders the need to communicate, and ensures the dissemination of new knowledge
- o Self-confidence is the popular term used for the size of the Self
- o The feeling of happiness – similar to the feeling of being penalized, or anxiety – is required to motivate (penalize, reward) a person to adapt.

Principal points covered in this chapter:
- introducing the elements FIPP uses
- changing Self-narrowing into Self-expansion via new cognitive schema
- broadcasting that schema

2. ARTS AND THE COMMUNICATION OF COGNITIVE SCHEMATA

Communicating cognitive schemata through art. * Comparing FIPP and Berlyne's inverted U-shaped model. * Cultural embedding. * Differences between kitsch, art and "art". * Detective thrillers, thrilling horrors and horrid horrors. * The artist as a communicator. * What are fashions, and examples of good teachers, speakers, and illustration? * Beauty defined.

The psychology of Art and Berlyne's model

Why is art psychology the first example mentioned in a book about FIPP? Because the whole of that model is rooted in art psychology.

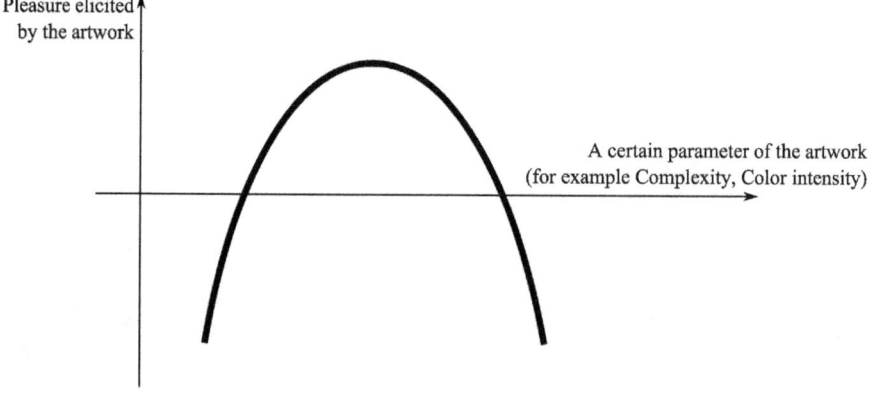

Figure 3: - Berlyne's inverted U-shape

Introducing Berlyne's inverted U-shaped model

An important phase in the evolution of art psychology began when D. E. Berlyne, examined the visual arts, and identified an inverted U-shaped curve that explained the connection between certain parameters of an artwork and the pleasure it provides; see illustration.

In brief, that connection is of a certain parameter – for example, complexity, the number of colors, or density – that elicits an increasing pleasure. Measuring this from zero, that pleasure seems to reach an optimal, positive point, after which it begins to have a negative effect, which can then become disturbing to the observer of the artwork.

The advantage of the Berlyne model is its elegance. However, the model has little or nothing to do with real art. Examining the arts from a practical, measurable viewpoint is a childish simplification, as the basis of art is strongly connected to the period(s) and culture within which it was created. Let us call this cultural embedding. The Berlyne model does not consider these connections.

The elegance of the Berlyne-curve model describing the pleasure effect, despite its disadvantages, seemed to offer an implicit foundation, which I shall later justify and prove.

Can we improve Berlyne?

The key issue is not to examine the intensity of a parameter, but to observe the distance between the cognitive schemata* of the artist and the observer. For example, in the case of a photograph of an apple, the photographer who sees the apple illustrates it the way we see it in two dimensions. In this case, we do not have to work too hard to understand the uniformity of the two schemata, as the distance is practically zero. However, if we look at an apple drawn or painted by Picasso, we need to make a serious intellectual effort to 'see' the apple, or to 'see' the apple the way Picasso saw it. Those who give up before seeing the apple loathe, or at least dislike, Picasso, saying that he only scribbles. They appear to give up before a new cognitive schema has been created. Catharsis did not happen, and they did not achieve a Self-expanded state. In contrast, retaining their Self-narrowing causes them to become angry. If they do not understand the picture, they would remain neutral about it.

In addition, what happens in an apple? It is not a unique experience, even if we add the effect of solving a puzzle; reconstructing Picasso's 'scribble' to a form. A further experience is obtained in that, by solving the puzzle, we have a better understanding of the apple, and the observer of a painting sees it more plastically than on a photograph. We see it almost in 3D, to the point of believing that we can smell the apple, as the apple's cognitive schema becomes increasingly activated compared with the activation effect of a photograph.

What happens to cultural embedding?

Cognitive schemata themselves are culturally embedded. So, to make a "correct" conclusion on an artist's cognitive schemata – understanding the artist's message – requires knowledge of the impulses and information that affected them. For this, we need to know the age and culture in which the artist worked, or works. For example, to understand a Renaissance painting, one should have a certain knowledge of the Bible, and the visual tools that Bible stories provide. This may communicate a message pertinent to the present, so providing us with a useful cognitive schema in our 21st century life. In addition, establishing these cognitive schemata causes Self-expansion.

Comparing Berlyne's model – which somewhat charmingly ignores the question of cultural embedding – with FIPP, we see that FIPP can explain not only classic visual arts but also any works of art or creation. For example, it explains the fun of tasting wine, when after some trials we can recognize the taste of spices and fruits within it. Or in reading a poem, when the unstructured cognitive schemata of the poet enter the reader's mind and establish new connections and schemata. Or in admiring a building, which connects the schema of the building to value or values it suggests, so establishing a new one; for example, the Eiffel Tower as a flexible, elegant, light but ambitious structure representing the French spirit.

Understanding the differences between kitsch and art, and high art and popular art

Using FIPP as a generalized Berlyne model, we can understand the difference between kitsch (worthless, or pretentious art) and 'high' art. The principal question with high art is that it is more difficult to understand. In contrast, as kitsch, and popular art, do not need intellectual effort to take them in, we realize that our efforts with higher art obtain a benefit. We can see that solving the mystery in an artwork – for example, where is the apple in the cubist 'scribble'? – is not an effort to see l'art pour l'art,[2] but enriches us by establishing new cognitive schemata. If we see a half-eaten apple after viewing Picasso's apple, we might perceive new associations with it. Whereas with kitsch, we need make no serious effort, and thus do not create cognitive schemata that can be used otherwise than in viewing a specific item of kitsch. So, kitsch does not enrich our knowledge or personalities.

However, we should understand that popular art can create new cognitive schemata. The difference between popular and high art lies in that level created by the new cognitive schemata. In the case of a comic, the new schema is created at a very basic level, usable almost only in the context where it was created. Whereas in a Bergman film, we might establish new cognitive schemata connecting with our whole life, being the highest level of cognitive schemata.

Identifying these differences between levels of our human life raises a question. On what levels do different types of art elicit their effects? For example, pornography and horror are said to gratify one's basic instincts. Detective stories are deemed interesting because of their ability to excite. These artistic forms continue to be increasingly popular, as they satisfy specific demands. But how do they satisfy those demands?

To date, most of our knowledge is a hypothesis on a particular genre satisfying particular demands. This has resulted in a process whereby we classify genres considering the general human or ethical value[3] of the demand they satisfy. Pornography and horror could be on the lowest level, followed by detective fiction, and on up to high art. However, even critics admit that true genius can place superior

---

[2]   art for art's sake
[3]   sex, eating, physical needs on the lowest levels; altruism, social work, self-realization on the highest level; compare with the Maslow pyramid

messages – those that are of more use in one's life than simple, targeted messages – in some of the genres classified as inferior. Edgar Alan Poe's detective stories provide such an example.

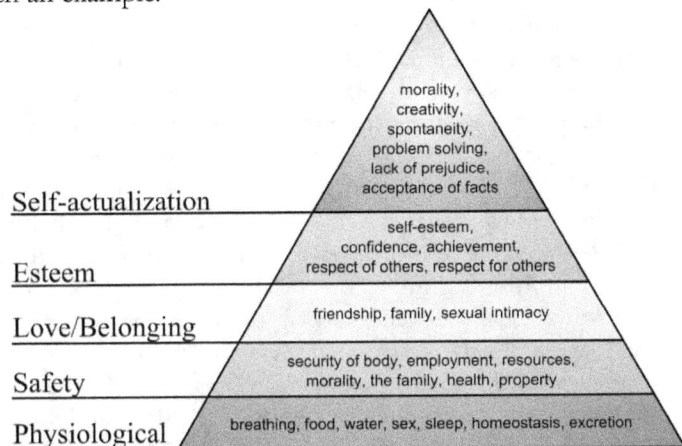

Figure 4: Maslow's pyramid and social values

Do these lower level arts cause an effect just by simply satisfying inferior desires? Even persons of high artistic repute might listen to rave music, read comics, watch cartoons. In the following, we try to determine the mechanism behind the effect of different art.

Detective stories

A typical detective story contains the following elements:
- o the description of the crime (or what can be found at the scene of the crime)
- o an investigator, who often reconstructs the crime and identifies the suspect via a clean, logical thought process, paying attention to details that a reader may have thought irrelevant
- o the enigma is solved, the guilty are arrested...

Let us translate these using FIPP terms:
- o the Environment is the crime. To begin with a big Environment, the crime is related to aggression that automatically increases the Environment's size compared to the Self; it is rare that a detective story is concerned with "who was it who saved somebody's life?" When we accept the story's framework – perhaps it occurs during the last century, or in an upper-class environment etc. – then our Environment is identical to the detective story;
- o from acceptance of the story's framework, the Environment begins to increase and narrow the Self. This process is described in everyday life as excitement;
- o the increase of the Environment is undertaken as we follow the detective's investigations;
- o the Environment reaches its maximum when we are close to giving up in

attempting to solve the crime;

o then, by receiving required pieces of information, we can create (reconstruct) the cognitive schema of the crime. If this is not possible, we then listen to the detective who reconstructs the crime;

o when the new cognitive schema was created, the Self regains control on the Environment – by retrospectively understanding how the information we had about the crime connects to each other – and this leads to Self-expansion;

o this Self-expansion, in itself, is a joyful state that compensates us for the effort spent during the Self-narrowing, perhaps when reading the book or watching the film. A further question arises: is this new cognitive schema usable for anything else? Perhaps one does not have to read a book in order to learn the techniques of committing a crime;

o there is a slight difference between solving the crime by ourselves or needing the detective to provide the solution. Solving it by ourselves creates a new cognitive schema, which leads to greater Self-expansion. In the second case it is the Self of the detective which is greatly expanded, and we are the first listener with whom he/she shares his/her new schema. The latter also creates a new schema in us, but the effect is usually smaller;

o an important point is that the more complex (but still understandable) the crime, so more logical steps are needed to understand or solve it, and so the greater Self-narrowing we tolerate, for which the reward is greater Self-expansion; however

o I have never read a detective story describing the Self-expansion of the detective...

It may be seen, from a psychological viewpoint, that this process has many similarities with problem solving.

Horror and Anti-catharsis

Catharsis

Before we attempt an explanation of the "beauty" of horror films, let us briefly familiarize ourselves with catharsis, one of the main concepts of ancient Greek aesthetics[4] and one parallel with the aha experience.* According to the Greeks, it is the basis of artistic pleasure when a story, (typically a tragedy) with a negative consequence – the death of the leading character – ends on an optimistic note; the tragic event serves to show a greater good on a more general level. For example, the hero dies, but his city is saved. The Greeks describe catharsis as an overwhelmingly positive event that strengthens people's morality.

How does this work? When a film does not end happily we are sad. Self-expansion is usually described as a positive feeling. Is there a contradiction here? The contradiction can be ignored if we take into account that a new cognitive schema is created. We realize that sometimes we have to lose something to achieve

---

[4]   the appreciation and philosophy of beauty

higher goals. Naturally, we are happier when we win without effort or loss. However, that is seldom the case.

The other cognitive schema that a sad or tragic ending provides is the establishment of order amongst our personal values. When watching a drama, we feel empathy with the main character, and try to guess how we would have behaved in similar circumstances. As the main character behaves according to his or her own ethics, so we have also to reflect on our own ethics. As he chooses, say, between his child's life and saving his city, or between his reputation and his team's victory, so our priorities are made clear.[5]

Pink Flamingos and anti-catharsis

To explain the cultural value of horror films in forming and bolstering schemata, a critique of "Pink Flamingos" might be useful. This film, which uses a technique that I term 'anti-catharsis', is concerned with making disgust limitless. Presented in a rather naturalistic manner, it seems impossible that most of an audience could watch this through to its end; I do not consider myself inhibited, but I could only watch the first third. The film centers on two mentally disturbed people competing to determine which of them can do something more disgusting than the other.

An example from the film: one of the main characters wants to have a child by kidnapping a woman, keeping her as a hostage, have a homosexual man try to rape her but, having failed, he injects his sperm into the woman with a needle. Later, they sell the child "produced" by the woman to buy drugs. Another storyline within the film is of a woman who weighs some 440lbs,[6] living in a mobile home in an incestuous relation with her retarded son. While shopping, she pleasures herself by walking with a raw chop between her legs.

I struggled to detach myself from the visual stimuli, while thinking of the twisted mind of the person who had written it. When I could take no more, I left the cinema. There then occurred catharsis. On the street were ordinary people I considered beautiful, and the ordinary weather seemed like the nicest day of spring.

What happened? I escaped from an extremely Self-narrowing state, compared with which even the ordinary outside world brought Self-expansion. The deadlock* was the moment I decided to leave. Even now, I consider the concept of the film wonderful. However, when I tried to watch it again, I could watch even less. This event made me realize that one can reach Self-expansion not only by starting and rising from the average level (by making superior cognitive schemata), but also by forcing oneself to concentrate on the most inferior cognitive schemata, and then the cognitive schemata of our everyday life. We could say that in this way

---

5   a colleague related that, when playing in a psychodrama, he realized that the success of – and everything to do with – his daughter, was far more important than himself. Until that moment, he would have been able to answer only theoretically that that was the situation. In the psychodrama, he also felt in his body that that was the case. That then became an axiom of his life, and so made decision-making easier as the priorities – at least concerning this topic – became clear

6   ±200 kilograms

nothing changes: we do not create any new cognitive schemata. That is not true: we restructure our existing cognitive schemata on seeing the beauty in our every-day life. The different perspective on our usual life is the new cognitive schema, which enriches the way we view our ordinary lives.

A similar experience occurred when I asked Scandinavian friends why they had moved to Hungary, leaving behind what would seem to an outsider a perfect country, with a functioning, honest society, a high standard of living, and so forth. The gist of their answer was: the Hungarian weather is heaven itself to us. Yet I want to go to Hawaii and the Seychelles.... So, I learned to appreciate our weather. On the other hand, the wife of a good friend had to move to Hungary from Israel. Clad in a coat in the middle of October, she said "Back home I could walk on the beach in a bikini right now...". In addition to my neutral opinion, the two further perspectives enriched my cognitive schema about our Hungarian weather: what can be heaven for a Swede is rather cold for an Israeli.

However, to return to horrors other than weather "Pink Flamingos" is an atypi-cal horror film: it is not full of blood and gore, and one is not scared all of the time. But the mechanism is the same: after we are frightened (or disgusted), our Self narrows intensely, we leave the cinema or switch off the TV. When in our warm, cozy room, or while stepping out into the sunshine from the darkness of the theater, we realize that we are safe and far from these mentally disturbed peo-ple. Our relief and appreciation then cause our Self to expand.

The same occurs with very spicy food. Eating it may initially be painful and cause discomfort, but when the effect is fully released our Self begins to expand from its narrowed state.

Valuable detective stories, horror and pornography films?

New cognitive schemata can be established on more than one level: an author can create new schemata close to those instincts of less intellectual people, and higher level schemata for those ready to use their intellect and learn something more.

An example of this is Shakespeare. In his time the theater was attended by peo-ple of all classes and ranks. Shakespeare was able to satisfy that range of interests and demands in the same play. For instance, Hamlet loved Ophelia (romantic feel-ings for ladies), it has many duels (aggression for men), but one's own schema can be enriched with further topics: family affairs, jealousy, politics etc.

As for pornography, the value of a film such as "Emmanuelle" is that, apart from the spectacle of naked bodies and sexual intercourse, it attempts to explain the power of feminine beauty and the different roles a woman can have.

An educated person, with experience of classical arts – Shakespeare, Goethe etc. – may try to protect others from kitsch and so-called commercial arts, seeing them as being inferior to the classics. I might also do this, but for different reasons.

Let us classify the artworks under three art forms:
o popular art: made for the masses for the purpose of generating profit for its authors (for example, action films, romantic novels, soap operas…)

o high art: which can satisfy the demands of the well-educated, high-IQ population (for example, Bergman, Goethe, Picasso)

o commercial art: which has some of the characteristics of high art, but with only a shallow message (for example, most Oscar winning films, such as "Titanic", "American Beauty" etc).

Popular and high art are fair deals, according to the model of cheat detection:

o popular art: a small investment – one only has to look at it – one reaches virtually no profit (no teaching)

o high art: a large investment – one must have preliminary knowledge to understand it, and, later, to consider it further – it provides a large profit and answers to major life questions

o commercial art: promises a big profit for a small investment, yet delivers only a small profit for a large investment. This is perceived as a cheat.

According to FIPP:

o popular art creates basic (low-level) cognitive schemata. Its pleasure lies in changing Self-narrowed and Self-expanded states quite quickly (compared with thrills, excitement)

o high art creates high-level cognitive schemata, which can be used later for creating lower- or mid-level variants. It provides both a better understanding of the world and greater self-expansion

o commercial art attempts to establish higher level cognitive schemata but, as it activates only low- and mid-level schemata, so it results only in low- and mid-level schemata. As the author knows that there is no new and clear high-level schema to communicate, it is like talking without a clear message; he/she cannot communicate a non-existent answer to a question. At the same time, however, it seeks to make these mid-level, rather tendentiously formed, schemata bigger than they actually are, by copying the visual world of high art. They hold out a promise of teaching more valuable high-level ideas, which they themselves may have not have, or only in an unclear form.

An artist is principally a communicator

The point of all art is that a cognitive schema originally created or held by some-one – usually the artist – is depicted in either aural, oral, or object form. Through its communication, that elicits a Self-expanded state in the mind of somebody else by establishing a new cognitive schema. This capability of artistic works to gener-ate Self-expansion explains why something, apparently without a practical purpose, has existed on Earth since the first human: the earliest art seen in cave drawings, fertility sculptures etc. In addition, the first artworks provided the possibility to spread those newly-born cognitive schemata that verbal communication was un-able to.

Figure 5: The Creation of Adam (Michelangelo, c. 1511)

To illustrate this:

According to the Bible, the first man was created by God shaping the human body from dust and then breathing a soul into his nostrils, the soul being the divine difference distinguishing objects from the living. By this process, the body of dust came alive, and the first man, Adam, was born.

To this point it is a story known by most people. If you had been there as an outsider, and could have recorded it on camera, but allowed to show only one frame of that film, which frame would you choose?

Possibly, the moment when something lifeless comes alive is the most important.

Perhaps Michelangelo was the first artist to realize that, if he compressed that universal event – on how human beings were created – into a single image, he would contrast markedly the divine, the living, with mere matter, the lifeless. Breathing – here, breathing soul into the body – cannot be rendered accurately in a still image, so Michelangelo sought a solution. Artistic freedom enables the visualization of a cognitive schema without the elements required of such a schema. So Michelangelo portrayed God breathing life into Adam by touching, a much more concise gesture.

However, where is the communication in this process? In Michelangelo's mind, two new cognitive schemata emerged to provide an intellectual solution:

o the possibility of depicting the contrast between lifeless and living by a single image of creation; and

o in connection with that depiction, the priority of touch before breathing.

The following cognitive schemata required to be communicated are united in one image by the artist:

o the difference between the lifeless and the living

o God's power to provide life

o the state in which we did not exist, and that in which we do

o the visualization of the process of creation

Supposedly, the image itself – as a cognitive schema – came to Michelangelo by an inductive process, as he was meditating on creation, lifeless and living matter etc. However, it is possible that Michelangelo came to this image through calculation, design, a process of trial and error, or by deduction.

I believe that it was by induction, as:

o induction is more a characteristic of genius than is deduction

o painters usually think in images rather than by logical exclusion

Whatever type of thinking he used, one thing is clear: a new cognitive schema was established. Regarding our model, as the new schema emerged, so Michelangelo felt the urge to communicate. He was motivated to share his new cognitive schema with others, which gave him the energy to physically create the picture.

In the process of artistic creation (physical realization), and technical ability (knowing how to paint, and how to convey one's internal pictures onto a canvas), connect with the quality of communication. So, if Michelangelo had not thought so much about it, the message obtained by observers would leave them with difficulties in interpreting and understanding the painting. Fortunately, in this instance we have a painting where not only the concept, but also its realization, is exceptional. Note in particular the solution in the structure of the picture: the hand of God barely touches Adam, so accentuating the tension.

Artists can excel in two ways:

o those people we call virtuosi, craftsmen or, simply, professionals, can communicate their cognitive schemata intensely. We admire how well these people can touch the substance of something; compare a good photograph of an apple with Picasso's painting

o they have unique thoughts and cognitive schemata about life that are rarely achieved by others. Sometimes, results are a consequence of the artist's different thought processes: musician think in melodies, poets in words, painters in pictures, and so forth. They can add something that makes our life more understandable, as Ingmar Bergman does in film

The reaction to an artwork is the process of incorporating the new cognitive schema. In doing so, we (the audience) establish the same connections, and thus the same cognitive schema, and then connect that to our existing cognitive schemata. Essentially, the received cognitive schema becomes part of our thinking, a part of our Self. It also must be noted that perception is not a unidirectional process. In order to find the proper place for this new schema, we have to consider the schemata around this future schema of ours. This is what we call cultural embedding: the surrounding schemata should be similar to those of the artist. Otherwise, the whole process leads to miscommunication.

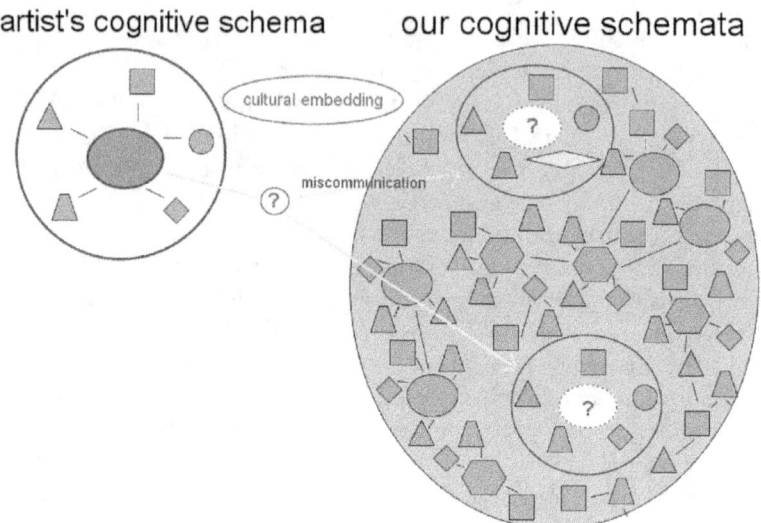

Figure 6: Whether we understand or misunderstand an artist depends also upon the correct decoding of cultural information

Therefore, with our knowledge of the Bible,[7] we complete the story, understand the picture, and so the new cognitive schema emerges. Those who do not know the Bible, or differ in their thoughts about the appearance of the first man,[8] will not understand the picture.

What is fashion?

It should be emphasized that Self-expansion is due to a **new** cognitive schema. After this new schema becomes well-known and accepted, it may begin to bore.

In discussing the spread of new schemata, fashion will inevitably arise. This rhythmical change from a new to a boring state, or at least one that is accepted unquestioningly, provides the following rhythm of fashion:

o a fashion appears,[9] with a newly-created cognitive schema behind it

o based on that new cognitive schema more, but lower level, schemata are created via deduction[10]

o when the new cognitive schemata have become known by the majority of the population, and there are then no possibilities for further deduction, the clothes or behavior based on this cognitive schema disappear, and a new schema appears and begins to spread.[11]

---

[7]   which functions as a common communicational coding/decoding system

[8]   for example, who believes that the first man was a monkey who could light a fire (evolutionist/atheist approach); or was born from the marriage of a jackal and the sun (in primitive cultures)?

[9]   for example, body piercings (at least in Western civilizations)

[10] for example in the beginning everybody thought that armless T-shirts in black were funny, then somebody tried armless T-shirts in colors

[11] for example, perhaps armless T-shirts with turtle-necks

Further examples related to the communication of cognitive schemata

The good teacher

We know that there are good and bad teachers. Moreover, we realize that a teacher we like may be disliked by others, so that there is no absolute good teacher. How can we conceptualize a good teacher from a psychological point of view?

To discuss this topic, let us ignore a teacher's personality, and that people prefer those who are similar to them or, in certain instances, diametrically different to them. More effective indicators are obtained by examining the qualities of a good teacher or lecturer.

As we already have a psychological concept of what people perceive as a good feeling in general – the Self-expansion – we can say simply that a good teacher is a person who elicits Self-expansion in the audience.

But how can a teacher cause – or create – Self-expansion? He starts by narrowing our Self through presenting the problem (our Environment becomes the problem) and the weight or importance of the problem (the Environment increases in size). He or she then takes us on a journey requiring attention and intellectual effort, showing us the path to the solution. Individually, we shape the new cognitive schema that he or she wanted to teach us.

An alternative to showing us the path is to drive us, so that suddenly, as when driving on a road, we round a curve, and our whole perspective is filled with the sea. We understand the solution in an instant, and have an aha experience. This alternative method can be called the "dynamic lecture" style: the subject appears to become increasingly complex, and then suddenly everything falls into place as the new cognitive schema emerges. Everything we saw before now makes sense. Moreover, we can reach conclusions by ourselves, when we realize a general connection that can be applied both to the present problem under examination and to similar problems. The ne plus ultra[12] of a good lecture is when a high-level cognitive schema emerges which has a general influence on our world view.

But what is required for that to happen? One must choose the speed and the level of cognitive schemata carefully. By speed, I mean that the Self-narrowing phase has to be well-designed and balanced: if it is too slow (too gently sloping), it is boring; if it is too fast (too steep), most of the audience will not be able to follow it, and will give up.

---

[12]   the highest, most profound position or state able to be attained

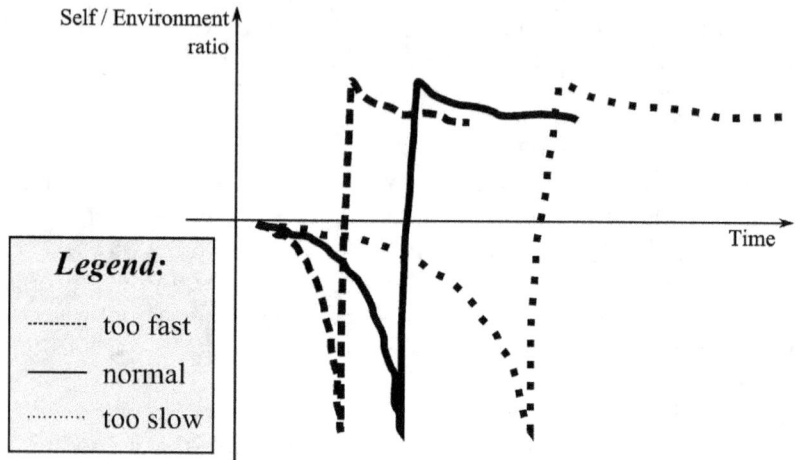

Figure 7: Different shapes of the FIPP-pattern, depending upon the speed of the lecturer

So, careful selection of the correct level of cognitive schemata is needed to ensure that the lecturer can use, can build on, the well-known, shaped concepts (cognitive schemata) familiar to the audience.

For this, the lecturer has to understand the limitations of the audience's knowledge. This requires a one-sender/many-receiver type of empathy. The lecturer can
collect information on both the speed and on whether he has chosen the right
level, by using the feedback from the audience. This feedback can have different
forms; from buzzing, rustling, chatting, through to being rapt or completely silent.
Or they are listening wide-eyed.[13]

The lecturer must also have reasonable targets. The lecturer has a chance to establish cognitive schemata within the audience only one or two levels higher than
those they had before the lecture.[14] New, but too low cognitive schemata, do not
elicit great Self-expansion, although occasionally it is necessary to broaden our
knowledge by learning listed items without any obvious structure; for example,
learning by rote the name of U.S. presidents, or the names of the states. Even
then, it is of greater interest if we first realize the common idea behind the list.

There is a difference of learning a row of random numbers, perhaps those in a
telephone directory, than by learning the names of different muscles of the human
body (anatomy). Although the latter seems also to be random, the names have an
internal logic. By learning them, a medicine student creates a cognitive schema of
the physical basis of the human body.

---

[13]   the phenomenon of being wide-eyed is pupil dilation, a side-effect of Self-expansion
[14]   it is difficult to explain complex numbers using only primary school knowledge

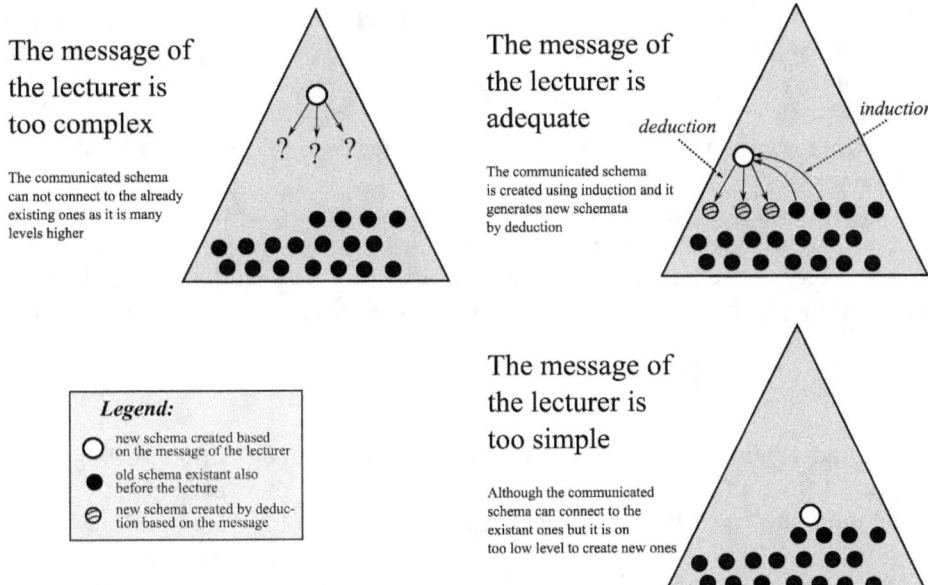

Figure 8: Different targets of the lecturer, and the effect on the audience of choosing these targets

If the Self-narrowing phase is overlong, people may give up, by physically leaving the classroom or turning their attention elsewhere. Another drawback is when an audience feels that the Self-expansion is not in balance with the former Self-narrowing.[15]

Occasionally, a lecturer is incapable of empathizing with the audience: their cognitive schemata are on such a different level that they cannot communicate. For example, where a university professor of mathematics explains summation to a primary school class. Even if he can do that, it is not good for either of them: whenever a teacher explains and proves a thesis, he rebuilds the cognitive schema in himself and experiences a small Self-expansion, or perhaps realizes some new aspect and so obtains greater Self-expansion. However, in the case of very low cognitive schemata, perhaps the most that the professor facing the primary school class can gain is the pleasure of imparting the methodology, the manner of his explanation, his examples, and so forth.

To return to personality...for a seasoned lecturer, choosing the proper level of cognitive schemata is mostly a conscious process. Thus, the selection of the target level may also communicate unconscious motives, for example, political views. So, those who deal impatiently with less talented students demand of the audience that it attempt to leap several levels, while understanding that only the most tal-

---

15   for example, when after a long explanation, the lecturer sheds light on a fact that was previously known to almost everybody

ented students will follow him, so indicating an elitist focus.[16] Those who take the less talented into consideration, and want to help their development – notwithstanding that that will negatively affect clever students – are likely to have sympathy with socialist or social democrat philosophy in everyday life. It is logical that the former requirement – of a leap of several levels – will be favored only by the elite, and that the latter will be favored by the rest.

This position is the same when calling students to account, or for the form, or quantity, or both, of their homework. We may even consider a personality trait: how much does the teacher prefer visual tools, or how visual does he or she think? Those students who have an auditory focus will dislike lecturers who always use charts and figures.

The good film

In the mid-1980s I learned that, if a director wants to avoid a film becoming boring and losing the audience's interest in watching it, then every seven minutes something new must happen; a diversion, exciting action, a new riddle, a new solution etc.

Intense attention cannot be endless in time. It will eventually weaken and turn to something else. Films that periodically give us new stimuli within this attention weakening period can be termed fast-paced; a master of this genre is Tarantino, or a better example might be the television series "24".

According to our theory, what happens in these fast-paced films is that the director changes the Self-narrowed and Self-expanded phases: the tension (Self-narrowing) and the solution (Self-expansion) change rhythmically (or at least periodically), and also new story-lines, possibilities, points of view. Anything new can be viewed as mini-paradigms* or new mini-frameworks, which cause further Self-expansion. Raising new questions[17] also requires new, lower level, cognitive schemata. The partial solutions to the partial problems give us small aha experiences, but previously they also unavoidably led to Self-narrowing.

From this point of view, a dramatic advisor has the knack of mixing these elements optimally. This can only be achieved by careful planning. We can become disorganized if the elements from different sources and of different intensity are not distributed and placed well enough. We can then either become disturbed by the excess of stimuli, or become bored due to the lack of sufficient stimuli.[18]

To sum up, a good dramatic advisor, together with a capable director and cameraman,[19] can play with the size of our Selves in a manner that is good for us.

---

[16] those who were unable to follow the lecturer might never catch up with the topic

[17] mini-paradigms

[18] as an example, a murder in an action film is a typical method for Self-narrowing. But when a negative character is killed in a long fight in which the hero almost dies, that will lead to Self-expansion. Love scenes cause Self-expansion, partially through empathy; we enter into the spirit of the character, how good it must be for him, kissing, being teased. Also, generally, love means the solution of a problem within the film, which anticipates the resolution of the respective conflict

[19] those who guarantee the technical realization, providing the same craftsmanship described in the Michelan-

An adroit admirer does the same with girls' selves and their self-confidence, varying compliments and affecting either complete attention, or indifference and neglectful behavior. These variations force the other party to be fully engaged and so they turn towards the admirer with greater attention; the chosen person's Environment is filled with the tactical admirer. She fears that she will miss messages that could increase her confidence, and that she might remain completely ignored.

In both cases (in film and courting) the key is not to let the Self of people rest **and** to ensure that the overall process will lead to future Self-expansion. So, creators and admirers have to meet expectations on two levels:

o inside the process, on different occasions there have to be several small Self-expansions ; and

o the whole process has to lead to Self-expansion. For example, the film has something to tell, providing a new cognitive schema, or a brief intrigue becomes true love, which is again a new cognitive schema.[20]

The good speaker

A good speech is based on similar principles. Although different in that it is less visual, far more intellectual tools can be used. The usual set-up is that someone stands on a stage and talks. They may use figures for explanations. The good speech has one or more clear messages for the audience. This message is in most cases delivered as evidence, a new cognitive schema. The greater the distance between the connected matters,[21] the greater the Self-expansion effect following the creation of the new schema.

There are different techniques to build up a speech. You can start with the general message, and later explain how you reached that conclusion. Another method often used by speakers is to repeat the path by which they reached the new evidence. This is similar to the Passion of Christ[22] being repeated by Christians each Easter. The advantage of this method is that many sub-problems, and the pleasure of solving them, can be communicated.[23] If the sub-problems are interesting in themselves, and if they mobilize the cognitive schemata surrounding the cognitive schema to be introduced, this may have a greater effect. This solution makes it possible for those cognitive schemata to connect more quickly with the new evidence – the new cognitive schema – as they trigger the schemata around the future schema, so causing increasing Self-expansion.

During a speech we have to pay attention to the harmonic distribution of evidence over a period, similar to the composition of a film, to retain the attention of the audience.

The function of presentation is to help the communication process by opening a

---

gelo example

20   the cognitive schema "Us" is formed in place of the cognitive schemata "You" and "Me"

21   for example, if it tries to place something in a political, social, or historical context, which is not expected

22   the last hours of Jesus before he was crucified

23   this supposes that the speaker does not state their cleverness in dealing with these problems in order to increase their own ego

visual channel to the audience as well as the auditory channel. As is known from the principles of Psychology 2.0, a good figure or diagram helps more in understanding than do ten pages of written material.

The good figure (illustration)

If we talk about the advantages of visual communication, let us examine, with the help of the FIPP, what can be said about good diagrams. The criteria for good diagrams are well known:

- o they must be easy to understand. It should display only one or two thoughts. In other words, we can say that it is focused
- o it is clear. Even the most striking illustration is worthless if we cannot identify the parts of it[24]
- o and it has to be simple. In attempting to understand a diagram, congestion[25] intimidates us

Distinctiveness can be achieved by considering that any new cognitive schema can be built only upon those already extant. So, the greater the number of existing and widely-used cognitive schemata we build upon, the better the basis for the new cognitive schema. If we want the audience to understand our illustration, we should apply to it as few abstract concepts as possible. We cannot count on newly-understood concepts, as they have not yet subsided.[26] Thus, regardless of how it would accelerate the process of building a new higher-level schema based on those existing, it is not advisable to use the newly-built schema unless there is the possibility of re-reading it, from a publication, notes etc.

Using color-coding is beneficial, especially if it fits the general notation.[27] We can rely on the use of Self-expansion colors (vivid, warm) to be used for marking positive things, and Self-narrowing colors (dark, cold) for details indicating danger or negativity, for example, illnesses, viruses etc.

The definition of beauty

Different things are 'nice' to different people, and so defining beauty is difficult. We can use the word "beautiful", although we may have problems with its definition. Maybe Kant best defined it when he said: "In general, beauty is what we like without interest." FIPP has an explanation for this phenomenon, and suggests a definition for beauty.

Let us attempt to understand why everybody does not like the same things, and why they call different things "nice". This lies in the differences of our cognitive

---

[24] however, a lecturer can use the technique of showing too much information early on in order to conceal the point of the lecture, and plans to return to an illustration later

[25] too much information density

[26] the new cognitive schema has not made connections with those surrounding it, and so has not yet integrated with the audience's knowledge

[27] for example, the traffic light use of red = do not proceed, green = proceed

schemata Even if we had the same cognitive schemata, they are connected differently. For example, the word "Madonna". An atheist or agnostic will associate the name with the musician; a Catholic will associate it with the Blessed Virgin; while someone studying for an Italian language exam may associate it with the word Madame.

Similarly, it is also important to determine those cognitive schemata that are active and accessible when a person is looking at a piece of art. That is why the surroundings are so important.[28] All of these circumstances have a priming effect. In psychology, priming means that the perception of certain stimuli predisposes us to certain answers and mental states in an ensuing situation.

A good visual example on priming is of two persons' profiles, which from another point of view might be seen as a vase. (This may depend upon what we have seen immediately before; having viewed a cup, we see a vase, or having seen a portrait, we see two profiles.) Priming helps to maximize the effect of an artwork. This is achieved by incorporating the cognitive schema within the same schemata that the artist had when he designed the piece.

Figure 9: Is this the stem of a vase, or a mirrored profile (white on gray background, or vice versa)?

To summarize, we can say that beauty is nothing but a cognitive schema – object, event, phenomenon, person, thought – which can be incorporated amongst our existing cognitive schemata, can totally connect with them and, as it is new, so elicit Self-expansion. The more cognitive schemata it can connect to, and the better its connection, the greater our perception of its beauty.

Principal points covered in this chapter:
- The formalized description of differences between
     -kitsch and art
     -commercial and high art
- the mechanism of artistic pleasure
- the mechanism of beauty's independence from genre
- FIPP can also form the basis of a new aesthetic.

---

[28] for example, when looking at a painting: is the museum quiet; silent; is the lighting good; what are the frames like; is the color of the wall appropriate to the hanging; is the building sympathetic to the piece?

3. THE RIDDLE OF PUZZLES

> Life; a puzzle, a riddle, a joke? * Self-expansion; the first steps. * Hooked by involvement. * If at first we don't succeed... * It can eventually - be done. * Mind games. * And if you don't like exercise? * Outsiders acknowledging Self-expansion. * Scientific and theological studies; a conundrum.

Introduction

Every day, millions of people invest considerable energy in solving crosswords, riddles, and jokes. Why do they do so? The punch lines of the silliest jokes, and the rewards for finding the solutions, seem laughably small compensation for the intellectual effort and time involved. Apart from the so-called "brain gym" effect, perhaps some internal reward system may be the explanation for this seemingly irrational behavior.

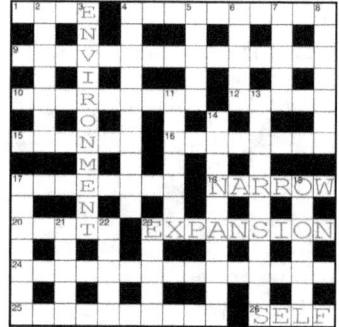

Another, seemingly irrational, form of behavior is that people submit solutions merely for the reward of seeing their names listed in the magazine.

Figure 10: An example of a crossword puzzle

The process of Self-expansion may be an internal rewarding system following the formation of a new cognitive schema. But when are such new cognitive schemata formed during the solving of riddles etc?

A good beginning - initial Self-expansion

According to the FIPP model, when faced with a blank crossword, our Self meets a small Environment. The empty grid, by definition, provides no information, and the clues are abstract until placed in their context and answered. Therefore, the state of preparing for a crossword can be characterized as an Expanded Self, similar to that when given a blank sheet of paper and allowed to do anything we want upon it: we can write prose, scribble, or draw a design. This can be observed in the excitement of anticipation in crossword puzzlers when receiving, as a gift, a puzzle book, or they buy the new issue of their favorite crossword weekly.[29] This phenomenon is full of contradictions, as receiving a puzzle book means the beginning

---

[29] such excitement is tempered, or even completely dissipated, if they see that somebody else has partly completed the puzzle

of many hours of work for no financial reward.

Increasing involvement

When somebody begins to complete the puzzle by writing in the first letters, they seem incapable of stopping. The more letters that are inserted (the greater the energy invested), so the greater the commitment shown towards completing the puzzle. As time passes, it becomes harder to continue, as there are no easy tasks left, for only the harder clues remain. Existing solutions define the answers to the remaining questions, which is a restriction, but also helps at the same time. We can therefore say that the more time passes, the greater the energy invested, and so it becomes increasingly difficult to leave the puzzle partially unsolved and our previous investment wasted. The pool of possible solutions, and the freedom to show one's knowledge, becomes increasingly smaller. This exemplifies the process of Self-narrowing.

If we fail...

Extremely difficult puzzles can defeat us: in cases when we overestimate our abilities, we give up, and admit to failure in a narrow state of Self. The puzzle – the Environment – seems to consume a piece of our Self: we realize that our Self lacks the ability we believed we had, and this leads us to try to adapt our mental representation of our abilities to reality. This process results in the alteration of our Self, similar to that when we lose weight; our body becomes smaller so that our clothes may need to be taken in. Similarly, if we put on weight; we may have to buy new clothes. As with our body, so our Self is not a fixed size, or shape. Practically, it means that the Environment won that battle with reality. On the other hand, extremely difficult puzzles can give us greater success, and an expansion of the Self, and can be worth the risk.

If we finally succeed...

As we have seen, our Self narrows during the solving of a puzzle. But what kind of object do we have in mind? Two objects may be taken into consideration, which often do not coincide:
  o finding the solution; and
  o "leaving no empty boxes".
Both result in the formation of a new cognitive schema:
  o in tandem with a funny picture or a joke, a solution in words is a cognitive schema itself; and
  o the homogeneously filled figure without empty boxes is a visual cognitive schema.
The formation of the new cognitive schema goes with both the easing of tension – the expansion of the Self – and with growing awareness that we can control

our Environment. Upon these is the imperative of communication, to share the new cognitive schema with others. This communication imperative was described in Chapter 1.[30]

Now we can return to the two questions posed previously: the "brain gym" effect, and "submitting solutions".

Brain Gym

As an everyday explanation, the expression "brain gym" means the 'training' and stimulation of cerebral nerves in order to keep them in good condition, similar to that of the muscular system. But what does recalling, for example, an Assyrian king's name, have to do with understanding a tax return? That is, does recalling historical knowledge from time to time increase our other forms – mathematical, logical – of intelligence? Presumably it does not, but then why did the concept of brain gym spread?

In place of Brain Gym

Indeed, there is some truth in brain gym but, rather than making the brain do gymnastics, it means the practice of changing Narrow and Expanded states of Self. That is, it allows us to experience those states without cost; that there is no need to give up on solving an intellectual problem before the deadlock, as we will be rewarded with the state of Self-expansion. Do those who have menial jobs that are not intellectually challenging – perhaps street cleaning, although that is socially valuable – attempt to solve puzzles and problems to compensate for their daily grind? Or not?

The maintenance of intellectual 'fighting spirit' obtains the additional benefit of solving puzzles, instead of the seemingly inconceivable advantages offered by brain gymnastics. This can be seen in the interpretation of brain gym, that says the brain does not become lazy, that it is ready to meet challenges when necessary.

To return to the relationship of an Assyrian king's name and understanding tax returns...common to both is the mental effort put into them. Independent of which skills we use, it helps us maintain that 'fighting spirit'. The effort to create structures, the step-by-step analysis, the search for connections and keeping the whole picture in view, are common to both of them. This despite recalling the king's name requiring the application of long-term memory, while a tax return requires logical ability.[31]

Why do people submit solutions to puzzles?

An economist would say that they do it for an anticipated profit. Yet how can this

---

Chapter 1, page 10.
[31]   not taking into account the many types of logic puzzle

explain puzzles that offer no material reward, only a mention in the next edition naming those who sent in the correct answers? People cannot earn their living purely by solving puzzles.

The explanation may be that the state of Self-expansion incorporates a spur, a motive, to share the solution with others. This imperative can be removed via the newspaper: the solution can be submitted to a disinterested party, and in this way the success – the new cognitive schema – can be shared with others. Sometimes people receive feedback as well, as when they see their name in the list of those who correctly solved the puzzle. This feedback causes the Self to expand further, by making the belief in the solution stronger.

Solving puzzles on a higher level

From a broader perspective, studying sciences, or explaining the Bible and theology,[32] are similar to the processes described above. By way of distinction, in those matters where the solutions do not end in themselves, they may form new schemata that could be of a higher level, in that they deal with the meaning of life, the world, nature etc.

Explaining the Bible is riskier, but offers more profit than does the study of a science. Small successes occurring during the process of study can be found in both. In explaining the Bible we need to synthesize, understand and then reconstruct huge amounts of material. Nevertheless, if we succeed, we can form schemata of the highest level: about the meaning of life, the existence of God etc. The risk is that these schemata, for some, cannot be used directly in everyday life, as they relate to the relationship of the person and God. On one hand that is up to them alone, on the other it is not a means of payment. Contrastingly, the cognitive schemata that result from studying a science – for example, a material, or a technological procedure – are of a lower level, and can be used directly in everyday life.

Sciences (excluding philosophy), with their smaller and practical results, contribute greatly to everyday life. However, they will never relate to the questions of the meaning of life: the invention of the n+1 type processor, or the theory of relativity itself, says nothing about our order in the world, or of the ways to be happy and to value.

Principal points covered in this chapter:
- motivation for solving riddles
- relationship between puzzle-solving, practicing science and interpreting the Bible

---

[32] as a series of structural analyses

4. SINGING IN THE RAIN AND ALTRUISM

Gene Kelly's WYSIWYG; What You See Is What You Get. * Humans: selfish, rational, hedonistic, or altruistic; can I help you with this? * Unthinking Self help. * Military morale, and mother and child. * Selfish genes and FIPP; a fit? * Communication imperatives on Self-expansion. * Martyrdom; does a Joan of Arc suffer Self-expansion? * No altruism, no Self-expansion. * New Environments, new opportunities. * Is stress infectious?

Why does somebody sing in the rain?

I may not be the only person who feels that there is something strange about the most famous scene in the film "Singing in the Rain": Gene Kelly sings and dances in a very good mood, as if the pouring rain did not exist or affect him. Usually, people try to keep out of the rain; they do not like to become wet and risk catching a cold.

So, why does this dancer sing in the rain? Our first guess might be that he is on drugs, or in an extremely good mood. FIPP explains this phenomenon with the common link between taking drugs and being in a good mood: that the singer's Self is expanded. The characteristics of Self-expansion are the strong communication imperative[33] to share the new experience – the new cognitive schema – with others. That communication of the new schema cannot be hindered by any discomfort in the physical surroundings. The dancer singing in the rain shows us how independent a Self can be from the physical reality it considers to be its Environment: rather than the uncomfortable weather, it is the social Environment[34] that counts.

The visual picture is clear: the singer does not notice, or ignores, the weather, as his message[35] is so important that he wants to convey it and make other people feel as good by using whatever means he has whenever he can.

How does altruism have an effect here?

The social sciences[36] formerly saw human beings as selfish, rational, hedonistic individuals, driven to maximize their happiness and pleasure level. There is nothing

---

[33] see Chapter 3
[34] with whom the person wants to share his new schema
[35] for example, that he is very happy or in love
[36] economics, sociology, psychology, philosophy

strange when we assist ourselves automatically.[37] We do not mind inconvenience to become healthier, or to look more beautiful,[38] or when we are willing to help others because we expect a reward in the future.[39]

Altruistic help, enduring inconvenience or even facing death to save somebody,[40] is exceptional from this viewpoint. This type of action is not based upon economic rationalities, or personal interests that could be scientifically or mathematically described. So, rather than the social sciences, it was evolutionary biology that first provided a clear explanation for the phenomenon of altruism: that at the genetic level, it ensures the survival of species by keeping personal interest in the background.

Compared with evolutionary biology, psychology has no clear theory about the mechanisms of altruism. In psychology, altruism seems to operate with a background reward system linked with empathy i.e. with the ability to live through another person's feelings, experiences etc. As the empathy link is also unconvincing, altruism needs a simpler explanation.

The explanation based on the FIPP is simple: when accepting the fact that we help ourselves without thinking, we have the right answer to the phenomenon of altruism. We must bear in mind that the Self is defined as a relative entity; so, in the foregoing, "ourselves" means not only 'us' but also the Environment attached to our Selves. Therefore, to paraphrase that sentence, when we are in a Self-expanded state – when our Self and its Environment are merged – we help our Self and the Environment attached to it without thinking, as we would help our own physical body when needed.

If the Self merges with its Environment, there is then no difference between itself and those with whom it has merged. If we consider the subjectivity of this experience, we can also explain altruistic assistance when those we help are not physically present when that altruistic behavior occurs. It is mental processes, not the physical reality, that count.[41]

There is a major weakness in the available psychological descriptions linking altruism with empathy. In these, empathy works only in face-to-face situations, where the 'helper' perceives the other person's feelings. For example, we help a child if it is crying, as we feel the same discomfort he or she is feeling. But what happens when physical contact is not available, and we see a mental representation of a suffering child, as with charity photographs of starving African children?

When Environment for a soldier means his family and country, he merges with and fights for them, even at the cost of injury or death, as he would do to defend

---

[37] we scratch ourselves when we itch, we eat when we are hungry

[38] we take bitter medicine to get well, or endure the pain that goes with cosmetic dentistry such as teeth whitening

[39] waiters who are very helpful in order to receive bigger tips; we 'lend' the neighbor some sugar which ensures that, when we need of something, they will feel obliged to reciprocate

[40] for example, giving money to beggars, doctors working in Africa and elsewhere pro bono, policemen, firemen, and soldiers, risking their lives to save strangers

[41] for example, the people for whom a soldier is fighting are not present at the actions, they are there only in the thoughts of the soldier

his own body. This explains the importance of soldiers' morale, the general state of mind, fighting spirit, commitment to victory and solidarity of an army. When morale declines, soldiers begin to desert, refuse to obey orders, or become less brave and more frightened.

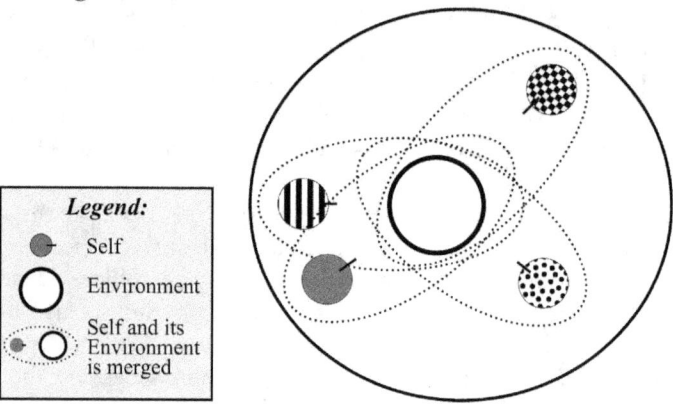

Figure 11: The soldiers with a common goal (same Environment)

Accordingly, morale is related to the level at which the Selves of the individual soldiers are merged with the same Environment. Being merged with the same Environment – for example, their home country – means higher morale, as they merge with each other through this common Environment, and so act more cohesively as a group.

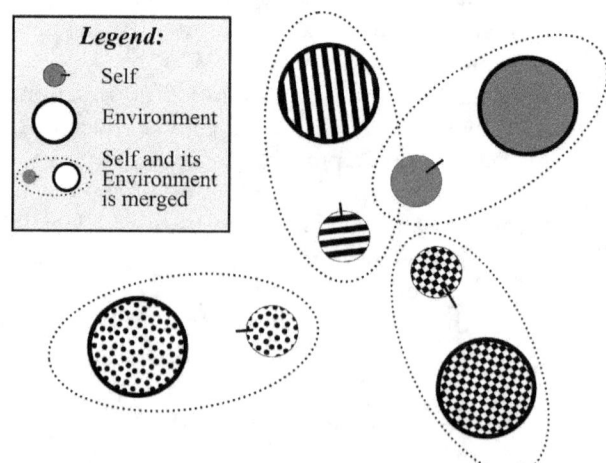

Figure 12: The soldiers focus on different goals (different Environments)

If the soldiers have no common aim, they will not fight with the same intensity that they would for themselves (for their own Self), and so exceptional bravery cannot be expected of them.

The merger of the Self and the Environment is related to Self-expansion and the dissolution of the Self's borders. As mentioned above, this merger, being a subjective/mental process, can take place between the Self and objects, thoughts and, especially, other people.[42]

The most thoroughly discussed example for the Environment-Self merger is the relationship between a mother and her child. Infants depend almost entirely upon their mother to feed them, keep them warm and so on. Accordingly, we can see that an infant's Environment is mainly its mother. The same position applies to the mother; the mother worries about and listens out for her child, to the exclusion of practically everything else. In psychology, this relationship is termed dual union. The unifying of two human beings has an extreme appearance: during pregnancy, when the bodies of the mother and her child merge and they feel similar stimuli, for example hunger, at the same time. It can be understood that when something hurts the child, its mother reacts as if it was happening to herself.

Altruism in the mirror of evolutionary biology and FIPP

Since Dawkins (1976), we have been aware of the importance of spreading solutions that offer comparative advantages to the other members of our species.[43]

This phenomenon is reflected in FIPP, in that new cognitive schemata must be shared with others, and the process of Self-expansion can be fulfilled only in a social environment. Two matters must be emphasized:

Our social environment comprises people who are important to our Selves for some reason[44]

The state of Self-expansion is possible only through sharing[45]

So, why does FIPP fit with the selfish gene model? The selfish gene model claims that it is evolutionarily worthy to pass on our knowledge to those with the same or a similar set of genes; only those genes which live in individuals with these characteristics survive.

FIPP describes the psychological obligation of this process. That is, why human beings living today (a species which has not disappeared since it evolved) cannot do other than pass on their knowledge to their close environment, and so help that

---

42 for example, a soldier and his rifle form a union, as do Einstein and his theory of relativity, a newly-married couple, a mother and child, and so forth

43 perhaps, if as a monkey I discover how to open a coconut, and I pass on that information to other monkeys, I increase the chances of my group being able to survive. In addition, my group may reward me; for example, by ceding control of the group to me (becoming the alpha male)

44 for example, if the key to our identity is that we are mathematicians, and that we wish to broadcast a newly-created formula, it is more important that we convince a famous academic than any number of schoolchildren. Or when we are in love – which according to FIPP means that our Environment is limited to just one person – we want to relate to that person we love, before telling other people, matters affecting us

45 for example, even if I write beautiful poetry, I will not be happy until I see it published and sold

small group of people with similar genes to survive.

A particular example illustrates that the state of Self-expansion can be experienced in a group; the smoking of a spliff[46], or joint. As the name implies, enjoying a joint is best when passing it around a group and smoking it together. Smoking a spliff alone can be accompanied by a bad, almost anxious feeling, related to the extreme expansion of the Self. Over-extension of the boundaries of the Self can cause an uncomfortable, frightening experience. Social environment has a crucial role in controlling extreme expansion, as communication with others helps to maintain our Self; feedback helps us to perceive (live through) the borders of our body and Self.

We sing in the rain...because we obey the imperative of communication

How do we adhere to the imperative of communication?

This is not an external imperative in the everyday sense. It is not a quick punishment following a negative deed. Rather, it is the lack of reward if there is nothing to reward, and a punishment if a positive deed is ignored. But what makes us do positive things?

The state of Self-expansion is rich in energy, which enables external resistance to be overcome when necessary, and to test, realize and spread the new cognitive schema. When this effort is prevented, frustration/aggression arise equal to that of the available energy, similar to high pressure steam becoming trapped and distorting or rupturing a pipe.

This explains, on a society level, the importance of the freedom of the press: enabling ideas to spread is socially valuable, and prevents people longing to communicate from being frustrated.

The imperative of communication is one explanation for the nervousness we feel when communication channels are unsatisfactory. For example, when somebody has important news for others, and wants to relate it on the telephone but the line is noisy. He becomes irritated, to the point of this turning into aggression and taking his anger out on the telephone itself.

Scientists and journalists are keen to publicize, to share, their most valuable cognitive schemata with the public. This phenomenon can be understood with the help of the process described above: they invent something and form a new cognitive schema; it makes their Self expand; and they are then eager to share it with their social Environment, that is, to publicize it.

Finally, an example, illustrating the importance of sharing experiences: "What could make a basketball fan very happy?" "Obtaining Michael Jordan's[47] autograph." "And what might then depress him most?" "If he could not then show

---

[46] A marijuana cigarette
[47] Perhaps the greatest basketball player ever; six-times NBA champion. The basketball equivalent of Pelé or Ronaldo in football

that autograph to other fans".

Altruism and martyrs

As we have seen, dissolving into the Environment leads to the state of Self-expansion: we think in terms of "we are" instead of "I am". In these cases, we maintain another person's or group's interest in view, our Selves dissolve in the Environment, and we enter into the state of the Expanded Self.

To better understand the mechanisms of altruism, let us take an extreme example; those religious martyrs who died to unite with the greatest number of communities possible.[48]

When younger I considered the behavior of martyrs, especially their pride and joy, irrational. With the help of FIPP, however, we can understand martyrs' particular logic. In martyring themselves, he or she encounters the highs and lows of humanity. This phenomenon can be described in terms of FIPP:

o the Environment is a valuable aim;[49]
o Self-narrowing is the fear of death;
o deadlock is the acceptance of death for a higher purpose; and
o that deadlock is followed by the greatest possible Self-expansion: a complete merger with the world, mankind, God, a brighter future, and so forth.

As martyrs' Self-expansion is so extreme, so their increasing energy is also extreme. This enables them to cope with extremes of resistance and frustration, which may be seen as superhuman to an observer.[50]

Fakirs and yogis also strive for a similar extreme of Self-expansion, but their methods are more conscious. The many ways of reaching the state of Expanded Self are discussed in Chapter 12 on happiness.

The lack of altruism, and Self-narrowing

We have seen that expansion of the Self induces altruism, and altruism makes the Self expand. But what is the relationship between altruism and Self-narrowing?

It had been thought that there are altruistic and non-altruistic people. The cause of this theory was the assumption that altruism is a personality trait independent of situations. In an experiment, students were asked the same favor,[51] some who were late for a lecture, others who had time to listen. According to the results, the situation (a student's state of mind, rather than their personality traits) was a better predictor of the appearance of an altruistic act. This experiment contradicted the previous assumption, that an altruistic attitude is a stable characteristic of a person.

Everyone can observe this phenomenon: people in a hurry are less likely to help

---

[48]   mankind, Church, God
[49]   for example, spreading a religion believed to be good for mankind
[50]   for example, Ancient Roman stories of religious martyrs praying after being thrown to the lions
[51]   for example, filling in a questionnaire

than those who are less busy, even if they have more resources. More surprisingly, we can observe in ourselves that, when we do not want to help (even if we could) for some reason, we pretend to be busy, suggesting that focusing on something else in our society exempts us from helping.

It is worthwhile comparing this observation with Self-expansion – merging with the Environment – an altruistic process described by FIPP, which is the opposite of this 'unhelpful' behavior. Our Environment is a well-defined thing[52] which differs from that of the person seeking help. The information from the person in difficulty disturbs us and we cannot – or do not want to – contact or merge with this different Environment. So, we will not become altruistic, because that would require replacing the current Environment with the new one. By replacing the current Environment, we risk reducing our Self. The bigger the current Environment, the bigger Self-narrowing we risk if we detach our Self from it. Meanwhile, the bigger the alternative Environment, the greater the opportunities for Self-expansion.

Being 'disturbed' means that the Self has first to make an effort to change its narrow state, and so redefine what it considers as the Environment. It would have to change focus, from the Environment that endangers the Self, to another person or situation. The larger we perceive our Environment compared with our Self, the less we can disregard it. For example, an impending deadline, another problem, a telephone call, can distract and attract our attention to the point that we find it hard to break away. The current and the alternative Environment compete with each other to be perceived by the Self as the larger, the more threatening, and the one which offers greater Self-expansion if controlled by the Self. The Self has to choose between the two Environments. That which is not chosen will automatically decrease the Self, or the potential Self-expansion which would have occurred if it had been taken under control by the self would be lost.

To better appreciate this, let us suppose that a businessman has to rush to a meeting, and will forfeit $1,000 if he does not arrive on time.

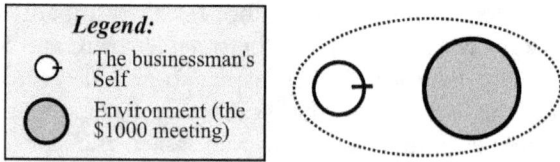

Figure 13: The businessman focuses on the $1,000 meeting

En route he sees a lost child.

---

52   for example, stock exchange fluctuations, deadlines, homework, commuting, are normal, everyday occurrences

In this position his current Environment is the meeting, and the alternative Environment is helping the child to find its mother or home. The subjective value of the $1,000 is the potential increase of the size of the Self. If he does not help the child, he has to relinquish the expansion of his Self that would have been achieved by taking the child to its parents.

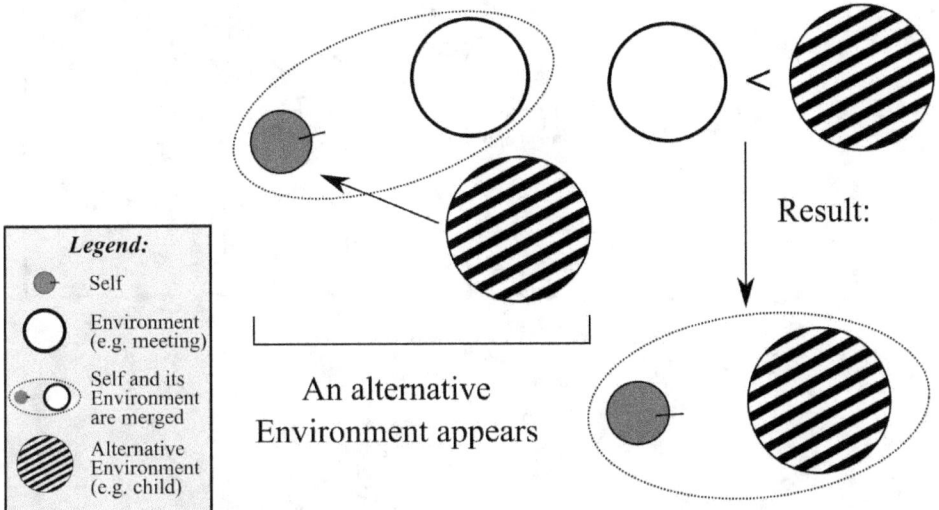

Figure 14: The businessman meets the lost child, and prioritizes helping against his meeting

Emphasized throughout has been the importance of subjectivity in FIPP. It is of key importance in this case; $1,000 versus the child looking for its mother. The alternative Environment – the child – can only be the larger and selected if it "attacks" using stronger stimuli than the Self of the businessman.[53] If these stimuli are not received by the Self of the businessman, then he would not help because the alternative Environment was not strong enough to replace the current Environment. In other words, by failing to help he risks losing a smaller part of his Self compared with losing $1,000. The bigger the businessman perceives the alternative Environment, the greater chance that he will help. Increasing the size of the Environment can be done by manipulating the picture of it through releasing stronger stimuli. This confirms our everyday experience, that it is not enough just to stay and wait for somebody to help you, one has to be pro-active in asking for help. So, the child has to cry more loudly to call attention to itself.

---

[53] for example, the child is crying; nobody is around; the weather is worsening and it is late at night

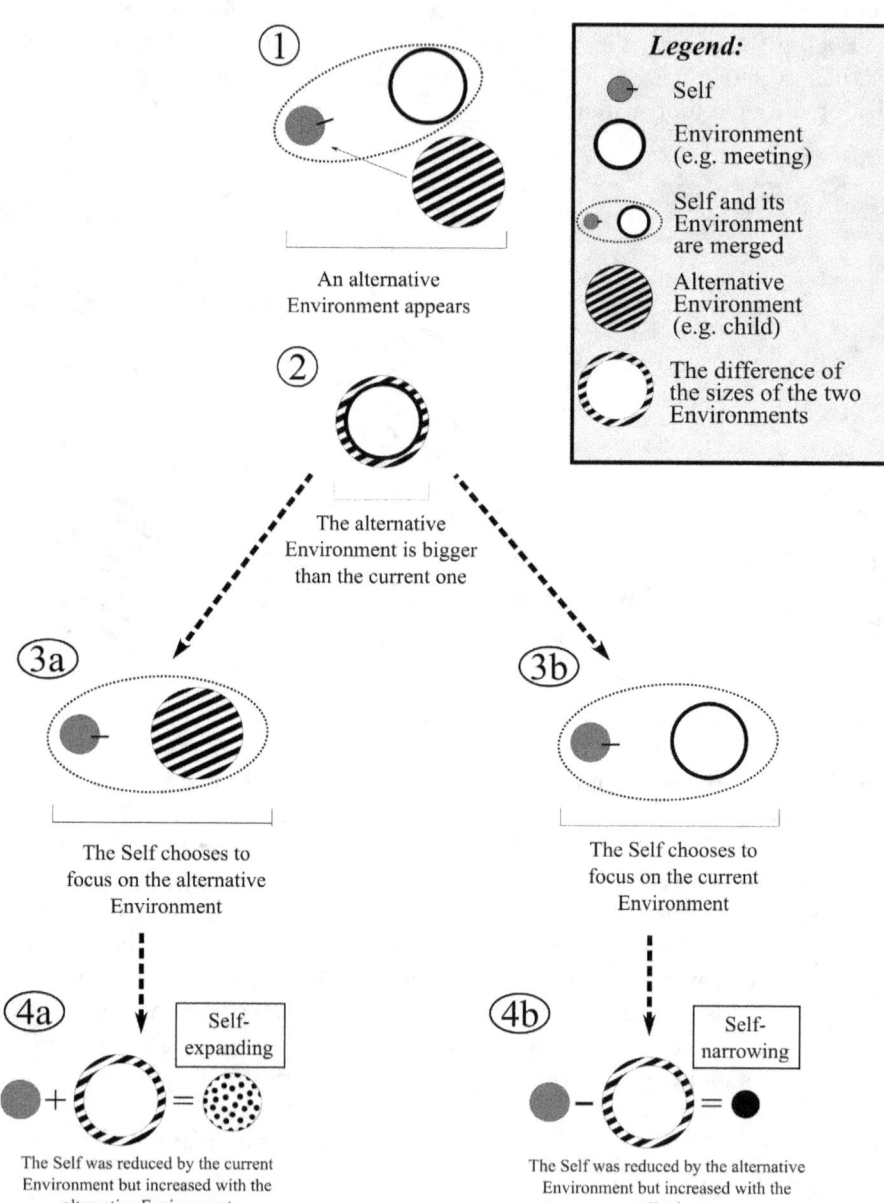

Figure 15: The decision making of the businessman.

To summarize, in decision-making the subjective profit or loss is what matters most i.e. the amount of the growth or reduction of the Self following the merging with either Environment. This shows that, if we need help, we must rely on more than mere facts; their appearance as an alternative Environment is required. Examples include the advertisement campaigns of different foundations and not-for-profit organizations, and advertisements in general: some of them promise Self-expansion by doing something, while others frighten or worry us into Self-narrowing by not doing something else.

One main advantage of the process described above, is that it explains why people in a narrow state of Self, facing a big environment, are less altruistic. Stressed people, facing a large, 'busy' Environment, need an even larger, alternative Environment, to attract their attention. Those who are in balance with their (smaller) Environment are likely to help, as merging with a relatively small alternative Environment can grow their Self, and so is of positive value to them.

Finally, the model described above also makes clear our dislike for people who are experiencing stress. Such people's Self is narrow: they do not appreciate humor; are not helpful; and are unsociable and bad company. The narrow Self has a close connection with aggression, which might provoke aggression or Self-narrowing at the people around. This is a further reason to avoid people who are experiencing stress.

Principal points covered in this chapter:
- understanding altruism
- restriction of the freedom of the press
- the joy of publicizing
- understanding martyrs and yogis

5. Spiritual Enlightenment: a complex phenomenon described in a simple model by FIPP

Enlightenment = ultimate and maximal Self-expansion. * Enlightenment and FIPP's pyramids of cognitive schemata. * Finding talent. * The enlightened and their environment. * One's induction to enlightenment, or by deduction? * Linking deduced schemata with others. * Enlightenment; have you got what it takes? * Enlightenment is where?

Introduction to the phenomenon of Enlightenment

Spiritual Enlightenment is defined as a religious concept that unites with the world by understanding the principal connections and driving forces of the universe. Although the concept itself primarily originates in Buddhism, similar states of mind are described in other religions and cultures. For example, in Christianity, "saint" is the word that describes someone so close to God, or to the universe, that that makes him or her special. In certain professions there are comparable concepts: those who attain the highest results or abilities in their field are called guru or grand master, a person able to answer all questions related to his field.

Throughout history, many people have attained this status, and were treated with great respect in their cultures. According to their own accounts, enlightenment is accompanied by eternal, constant happiness and calmness, while earthly, everyday matters lose their apparent importance.

The similarity between enlightenment and maximum Self-expansion, which comes after the establishment of a top cognitive schema that integrates all knowledge available to the person, is noticeable. We will now examine why these two states are the same.

How does enlightenment accord with the concept of FIPP?

The cognitive schemata of enlightened people

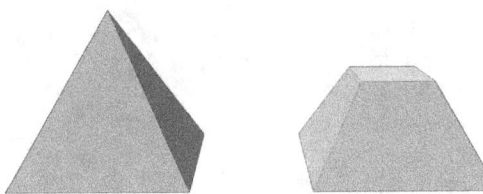

Figure 16: Pyramid and frustum of pyramid

To understand enlightenment from the viewpoint of FIPP, we need to keep the hierarchic construction of cognitive schemata in view. In the following, imagine the cognitive schema's hierarchy as a pyramid, where each building block of the pyramid is an individual cognitive schemata. The top of the pyramid indicates the cognitive schema, the so-called top-schema which integrates everything. Not all pyramids are complete: some frusta of pyramids[54] indicate all of the people who did not succeed in integrating their knowledge in a connected system throughout their lives; namely, they did not achieve enlightenment.

In the pyramids of cognitive schemata, it is interesting that every upper-level cognitive schema contains the lower-level cognitive schemata in an integrated way. In conclusion, the top cognitive schema has to contain the complete cognitive schema hierarchy i.e. everything that the person knows.[55]

Ignoring for the moment the concept of cognitive schemata, how can we erect, in the most efficient way, a pyramid to be

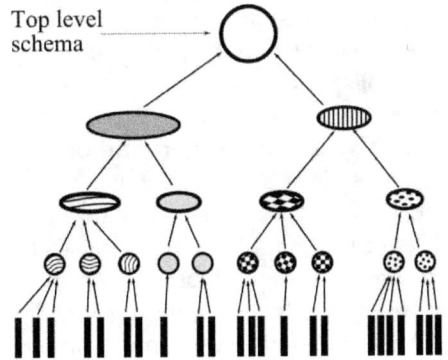

Figure 17: The top-schema integrates everything

---

54   the remainder of a pyramid after the topmost part has been cut off
55   this is similar to the CEO of a company who is aware of all the information known collectively by his employees

both the most stable and the highest?

One possible solution is a tall pyramid having a small base. This would mean reducing our level of aspiration, as a pyramid with a small base requires less material and construction time. However, it is less stable, and precludes the possibility of building a high structure. This pyramid with a small base can be seen in tandem with the enlightenment of those who live in an environment poorer in information, for example, on the top of a hill, in a hidden village, or in a monastery. Achieving enlightenment is easier for someone who has been partially isolated all his life from the outside world, since he has less cognitive schemata; for example, he may not

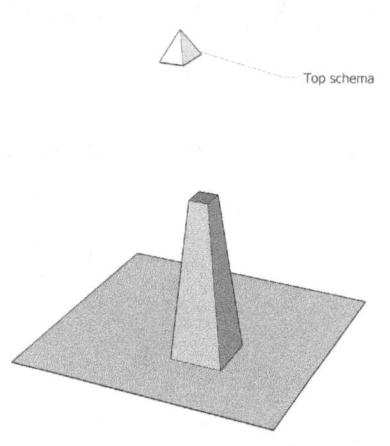

Figure 18: A pyramid built on a small base and the level of enlightenment (with white)

have heard of or seen drug dealers and gang warfare. Therefore, it is easier to integrate those few schemata.

Another possible strategy is to build a pyramid asymmetrically. This reminds us of the strategies of specialists in a narrow subject area with no other interests who, although they may have many cognitive schemata, develop in only one field, albeit one in which they achieve outstanding results. Nevertheless, this raises the question whether the pyramid collapses if it is not correctly propped up. Can such a person cope with impulses different from those of his profession? A mathematician may find social relationships extremely difficult to comprehend or cope with. An altruistic social worker may miss out on certain possessions or pursuits as he does not care so much about money.

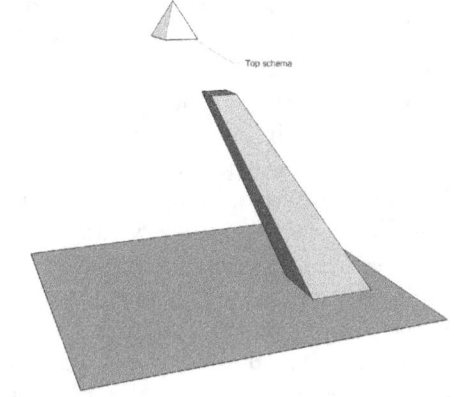

Figure 19: Asymmetrically (thus unstable), but high pyramid

The most reliable strategy may be not to build a perfect pyramid, but to shore up and surround our main pyramid with many sub-pyramids. This is the approach adopted by different school systems to promote the improvement of general knowledge. Apart from creating noticeable Self-expansion, general knowledge offers a chance to understand in which field the cognitive schemata establishes quickest, and so to identify a person's particular talent. Another effect of general knowledge is that it forms a bridge with other lower-level cognitive schemata; this bridge supports the main interest, enabling it to develop the Self to a much higher level.

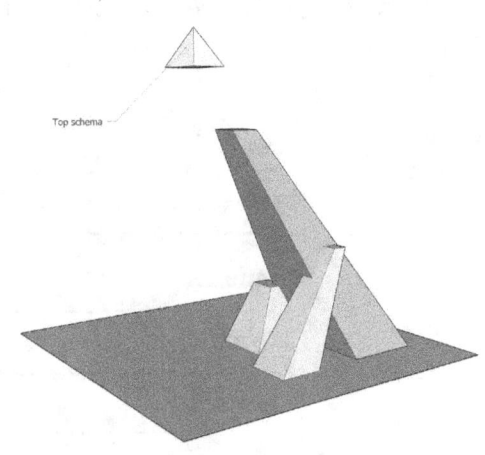

Figure 20: An asymmetric pyramid supported by smaller asymmetric pyramids that enable it to grow

The Self and the Environment of Enlightened people

Unification with the universe is a major phenomenon within Enlightenment. Those who reach this state feel themselves as part of the universe, and are unable to divide themselves from the outside world. They experience the world without mental pre-processing, so no new schemata are born, as all stimuli reach those schemata they are intended for.

This phenomenon can be described using FIPP terms, as the boundary between Self and Environment has disappeared. As all schemata that can exist have been born, there are no more conflicts within the perceived entities, and there is no need for restructuring anything within these cognitive schemata. Everything has been completed.

Emotionally, this leads to a calm that can be perceived as depression. The calmness/depression arises in that Self-narrowing and Self-extension have no place in the future. The Self is unified with the Environment, so there is no more fear from the possibility that the Environment will destroy the Self, as the two entities no longer differ. Lack of fear and anxiety is also a typical description of an enlightened person's state, and can also be explained by the irrelevance of Self-narrowing. The enlightened state is observed to be indescribable, in that as a top-level schema, it is not necessarily a verbal construct that cannot be translated into words, as words depict far lower-level schemata. Therefore, as this top-level schema cannot be translated into schemata that are available to ordinary people, so it cannot be communicated.

How does enlightenment happen according to the FIPP?

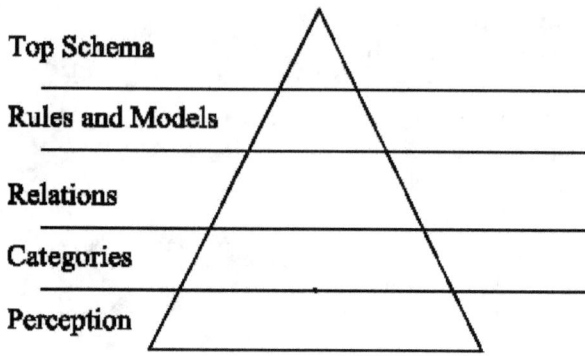

Figure 21: Different levels of complexity within the pyramid

On the lowest level of the pyramid of cognitive schemata, the most basic elements of stimuli from the outside world can be found; colors, shapes, etc. It is upon these that the categories and concepts that represent objects and people are built. Upon these categories we find the similarities that describe connections between objects and people, which become increasingly complex as we proceed to higher levels. Attaining a higher-level cognitive schema happens through induction; downward conclusions take place through deduction. Induction is the process whereby the Self finds a connection between two or more discrete cognitive schemata, and establishes a new, higher-level, cognitive schema. The process of deduction occurs where a higher-level schema combines with another schema, yet the new schema that emerges is of a lower level.

An example of induction: a basketball is spherical, a table-tennis ball is spherical, a football is spherical. The conclusion: all balls are spherical.[56]

An example of deduction: what shape can a baseball have? Since it is a ball it must be spherical. In this case, the baseball as another schema connects with the higher-level schema (ball).

Due to their nature, the stimuli and concepts that reach people form groups: visual cognitive schemata, such as colors, are different from musical schemata, for instance a tune. These groups can be found at different places in the base of the big pyramid, and they themselves form smaller pyramids. For example, Mozart had an extremely high musical pyramid with a wide base, while Einstein, although also having a high musical pyramid – he played the violin well – had a higher and wider physics pyramid. This did not mean that either of them had to have a large pyramid connected to, for example, swimming.

---

[56]   of course, there are always exceptions, such as the rugby ball

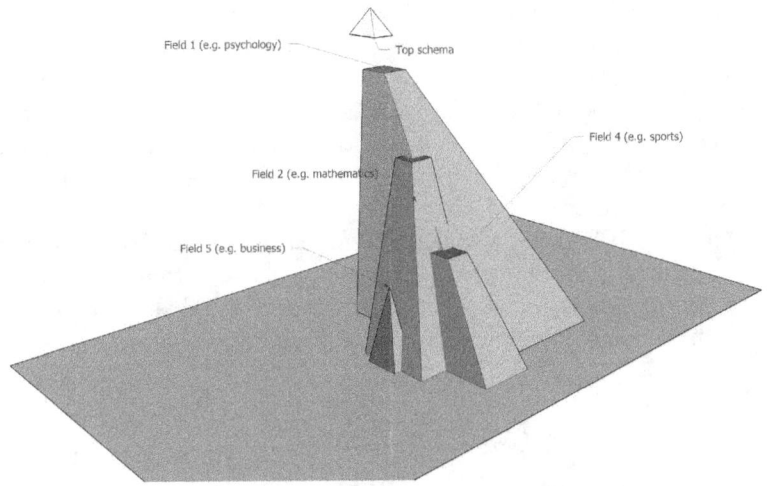

Figure 22: If its neighbors are also high, a pyramid can grow much higher

Schemata are interesting in that these pyramids can become mixed after awhile. A mathematician might find mathematical connections – rhythms, beats per minute, wavelengths, harmonic theory, note ratio et al – in music. Or the manner in which the results of biology influence our vision of society, as happened with the adoption of Darwinism.

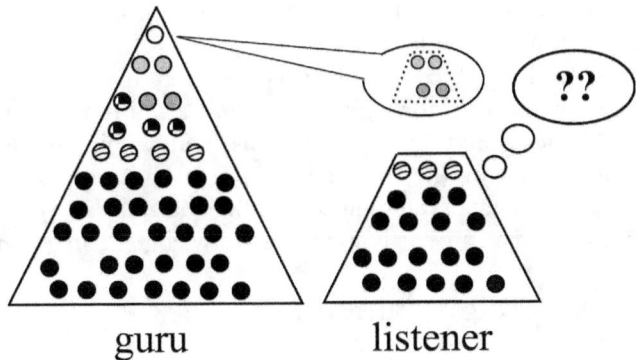

Figure 23: It is hard to understand a guru

We have previously mentioned one characteristic of enlightenment...that in the enlightened person's mind, everything becomes connected with everything else and a simple pattern, the highest level cognitive schema, explains everything they know. Since the top cognitive schema is built on cognitive schemata immediately below it, which are equally unknown to – or identified differently by – other people, he is not capable of communicating his top-level cognitive schema, as in the minds of others there are no adequate/relevant cognitive schemata that they can build upon. Moreover, it is not at all sure that this top-level cognitive schema can be expressed in words. For example, it is possible that a top-level "general" tune explained everything about life to Mozart, and tunes cannot be translated into words. It is said "it's easy if you know how" of people who find "it" easy, as they have a higher-level cognitive schema, as well as all those beneath it, and so everything is self-evident to them.

According to the FIPP, the way to enlightenment is to establish extremely high-level cognitive schemata in a certain field (sport, science, art etc.), which can later connect with the top-schemata of other pyramids through deduction. Thus, all the schemata of the person will be integrated in one schema, the top-schema.

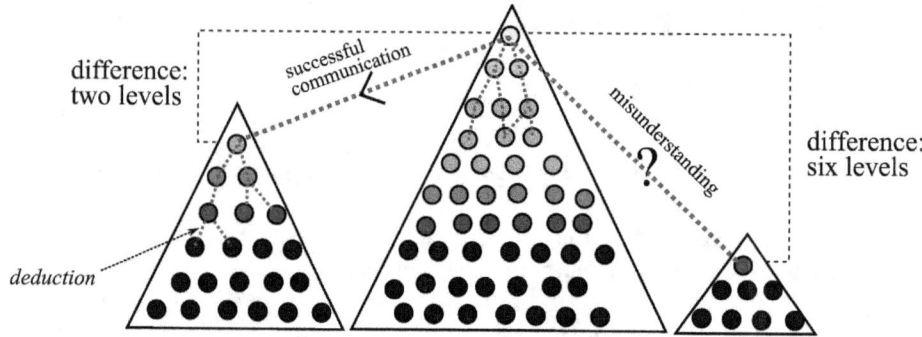

Figure 24: Top-level schema can only connect to schema no more than one or two levels lower

In order to make this possible, the favored schema cannot be many levels higher than those surrounding; for example, the second highest schema. The reason: that although through deduction we can also make schemata at several lower levels, very large gaps cannot be bridged through deduction. As an instance, let us assume that Boris Becker knows everything about tennis, and within tennis he has a schema, which would explain all the connections. But if he is only on the level of addition and cannot understand multiplication, then he will have difficulties in connecting his tennis schema with his incomplete knowledge of mathematics.

How do we attain enlightenment?

From a general viewpoint, the way to enlightenment does not differ from normal life. Schemata are also established one after another, and so increase the height of our pyramids. The difference lies not in the nature of the process, but in its intensity. This depends upon:
   o a question of talent
   o the choice of the method

Talent and enlightenment

Perhaps it is not surprising, though rather undemocratic, that enlightenment cannot be attained by everyone. To be able to establish a top-level schema, many schemata must be established beneath it. How many depends upon how much information is found at the basic level, and which has to be integrated.[57]

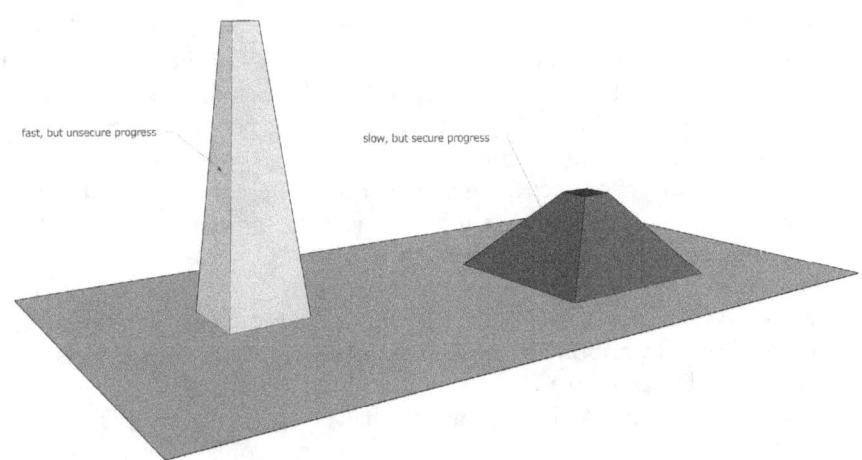

Figure 25: Some progress quickly in a field, others query – and check –everything

The question is: at what speed can these various schemata be established. It seems obvious to assume that, if someone is talented in a particular field, he can build the pyramid of that field quickly. This matches the observation that talented children learnt much more quickly the basic-level schemata of the field they later became extremely talented in. Mozart learnt the piano and began to compose at a much younger age than did his contemporaries with general musical talent. Moreover, as the frequency of establishing new schemata increases, so too does the frequency of Self-expansions. Engaging in a particular field that fits him enriches a child with positive feedback. In the meantime, this phenomenon also serves as a selective function, both in the choice of profession and of talented children. Those who do not have a genuine sense of achievement (Self-expansion) in certain fields will, sooner or later, give these up to benefit from what they are good at. Perhaps basing this on the presumption that we are born with different brains sounds particularly unscientific. However, we shall expand upon this later.

Within a personality, the degree of risk-taking and motivation for success or, in-

---

[57]   cf. a hidden village vs. a city's wealth of information; a caveman's vs. a 21st-century man's knowledge

deed, sensation seeking, affect the speed of acceptance of newly-born schemata. Some people are satisfied with a mere intuition of setting out on the right way, and take one step forward. Others (using deduction) check two or three times if the new schema covers the reality well enough. Checking is time-consuming, although it provides greater safety. The more schema there are, the safer the basis from which to step up onto a higher level.

Which methods lead to enlightenment?

A simple recipe cannot be described, as each and every person has their own way of shaping their top-level schema. As we have seen, those who achieve enlightenment have attained a high level in a particular field. This seems to be a criterion for reaching enlightenment. However, it is clear that it is not enough to be good in just one field, as we cannot then integrate everything. To achieve enlightenment, sooner or later we must connect the field we have mastered with the other fields of life, as the definition of enlightenment is that nothing can remain unintegrated.

It is also characteristic of the search method that:

o it has to cope with the frequent Self-narrowing – occasionally of a severe nature – that is a natural result of frequent restructuring of the schemata; and
o it has to deal with nobody being able to assure you that your efforts will lead to success (enlightenment).

So, continual uncertainty will accompany that effort. In sport, this appears in a spectacular and concentrated form: there are many professional cyclists in each country, but only a few from one country – its elite – will represent it at the Olympic Games. The uncertainty of whether there is a chance of becoming one of the elite, and whether it is worth putting so much effort into training, can only be overcome with coping strategies. Here, the role of personality again arises, not only in choosing the tempo, but also in providing diligence, persistence, bearing and Self-narrowing. All these are matters in which personality has an important role in connection with attaining enlightenment. That is why it is not incidental that people who want enlightenment do not care only about creating schemata, but previously – or concurrently – they prepare their personalities for resisting difficulties until reaching enlightenment, no matter how long that might take.

It is important to note that an enlightened person will not know the answer to everything. His knowledge will not be immense and limitless. Rather, he will be aware of life, human motivation and behavior, and his own principal connections. He will have a deep understanding of the regulation of the universe. It is similar when, in understanding the concept of gravity, we do not only understand why the apple falls on our head, or why the planets move as they do, but perhaps also why there is attraction between people. That he realizes that two people can look for each others proximity, or that there are certain central persons – Royalty, "celebrities" – around whom others circle, just as the Earth moves around the Sun determined by the laws of gravity.

Principal points covered in this chapter:
- understanding Enlightenment
- the pyramid structure of cognitive schemata
- the induction, and deduction, of schemata

6. UNDERSTANDING PROBLEM SOLVING USING FIPP

The activation, selection, application, and creativity of, cognitive schemata. * Their ability to problem-solve...and cause problems by interference. * Breaking down schemata. * Manipulating their parts. * Solving problems; possibilities or impossibilities? * Schemata and their 'children'. * The hunger for problems...and Self-expansion. * Self-confidence; true or false? * The narcissistic Self.

The role of cognitive schemata in thinking

Considering that, besides Self and Environment, cognitive schemata are important parts of the basic concept of FIPP, the FIPP model is particularly applicable in describing both the process of thinking and, within that, the process of problem solving. Cognitive schemata are not merely the building bricks of thinking, but more; they are the leading characters in new thought processes. Thinking is nothing other than the manipulation of schemata. Considering how many aspects of thinking – for example, memory, intelligence, creativity – are studied by psychology, this statement seems to oversimplify matters. However, if we examine it more closely:

o we can look at memory recall processes as the establishment, more precisely the activation, of a cognitive schema;[58]
o we can consider intelligence as choosing and applying the proper schema; or
o creativity can be seen as the establishment of a new cognitive schema by restructuring or combining – or both – those we already have.

I believe that these few examples demonstrate the relevance of cognitive schemata in understanding mental processes. As the workings of cognitive schemata will be described in more detail in Chapter 10, let us return to problem solving.

Problem solving described with the concepts of FIPP

FIPP attributes every problem to having two or more cognitive schemata that interfere with each other – neither or none of which describe the outer world properly – so that we cannot choose between or amongst them. This conflict generates the essence of our problem; the feeling that, at root, our schemata (or at least one of them) are useless, or our perception is wrong. This is a worry, and impels us to act and deal with the situation as a problem.

---

[58] cf. recalling data from memory

In order to demonstrate this approach, let us imagine the opposite of the situation described in the former paragraph, namely, a problem to which:

o a cognitive schema is the solution;[59]

o there are two non-interfering cognitive schemata as a solution.[60]

What then happens?

If a certain cognitive schema is the solution, then it describes the reality properly; there is nothing left but to use it, and there is then no problem.[61]

If two schemata that fit with each other are needed to describe reality, these two integrate quickly. Again, there is nothing left but to use it. And, again, there is no problem here.[62]

A problem as the interference of cognitive schemata

We can accept that a problem is nothing but the conflict of at least two schemata. For the sake of simplicity, and as the processes are the same, let us disregard the possibility of more than two schemata.

Hereafter, we can consider the process of problem solving as the constant growth of the Environment – composed of two interfering cognitive schemata – at the cost of the Self. The growth of the Environment derives from our increasing knowledge of the lower-level schemata which form the basis of the two schemata in discussion, and attempting to match them by breaking them down into increasingly smaller pieces. Different conclusions arise from this process description:

the process works well if:

o we can identify the schemata

o we identify the constituting schemata properly; and

o we manipulate an increasing number – at increasingly lower levels – of cognitive schemata, and to do so we have to suppose that the mind has a processing capacity

To make this clearer, let us examine the two principal results.

Partial schemata: dividing the schema into parts

In order to divide an upper-level schema into its correct parts, we must properly identify its constituent parts.[63]

---

[59] 'I am hungry, there is food in front of me'

[60] 'the door is locked; I have a key; and I want to enter'

[61] 'I begin to eat'

[62] 'I open the door with the key, then I enter'

[63] It is similar to a butcher cutting up a carcass; if he did not know the individual parts of its body, he would end up with strange, literally disjointed, cuts of meat

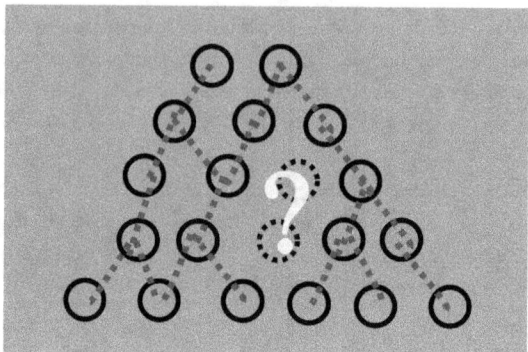

Figure 26: Missing schemata

This phenomenon arises as a schema could also be established in such a way that not all the schemata beneath it exist.[64]

The characteristics of the constituent schemata play a leading role when we divide the superior schema into parts. For example, its stability, how accurately it has been checked, how many other schemata it is connected to, and how unambiguous the connections are, both of themselves and in relation with the other schemata.

This is the difference between 'schools' and schools: accountancy is taught just as well at a 'lesser' college as at Harvard. While on Harvard, the connections between schemata that are presented have been thoroughly verified, and their clarity has been proven, in the 'lesser' college there is only surface order, as between the knowledge parts there may be contradictions. When a simple accounting exercise has to be undertaken, probably both courses are good enough to provide that capability. However, producing the annual financial report and accounts of a major corporation may result in dissimilarities.

The other phenomenon where partial schemata come to the surface is in teaching. Explaining what it is they do, and how, may provide a serious difficulty for people. For example, Lance Armstrong[65] explaining how to steer a bicycle, or what to do with the upper body when somebody is about to fall to the right. In order to convert these movements into words, he has to divide the movements into parts.

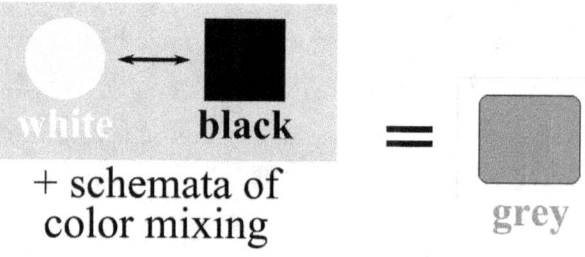

Figure 27: The schemata of color mixing helps solve the conflict between white and black, as it results in gray.

---

[64] such is the case of which people make jokes; for example, when someone miscounts 7 × 8, and says that he was absent from school the day they learned it

[65] multiple Tour de France winner

However, it often happens that other schemata help to solve the problem: sometimes it is not possible to integrate two interfering schemata, no matter how much we dissect them, but a third schema can make a threefold connection between them. However, to do this, a third schema has to exist, and somehow, by inserting the other two schemata, all three have to connect. For example, when resolving the opposite of black and white, they are integrated by the schema of color mixing[66], as different shades of gray.

The manipulation of partial schemata

Dividing a superior schemata into its constituent parts is not enough in itself: we must try to fit them to each other in order to make a new schema. To do that, we have to store the separate sub-schemata and be able to manipulate them. For the moment, let us disregard the speed of manipulation, as this affects intellectual performance. Let us also disregard the strength of the connections amongst the schemata, to which detachment (the speed of detaching) of the schemata is inversely proportional.

Schema 1

Schema 2

Schema 1 and 2 destructured

Figure 28: More space is needed to manipulate the sub-schemata

The phenomenon is similar to having two unique puzzles, from certain parts of which a new one can be formed. The size of the surface we work upon can make a difference.

In this example, it is the measure of the working surface, disregarding the num-

---

[66]   or rather by the schema of light intensity

ber of manageable schemata, that shows a strong connection with solving intellectual problems. In psychology, working memory, or short-term memory, is the relating term. But as mentioned previously, the strategy,[67] speed,[68] and the strength of connections,[69] all play a serious role in a person's intellectual performance within a certain situation.

Description of Problem Solving

Let us now examine the steps needed to describe problem solving. The problem can be categorized in two groups:
   o when the cognitive schema, meaning the solution, is available to the person
   o when the schema, meaning the solution, has to be established
Another possibility is of a problem having no solution, but this fact is unknown to the person.

The non-existent solution

Before concentrating upon problem solving, let us deal with the non-existent solution. A problem can be unsolvable:
   o for a certain person;[70]
   o if it is excludable according to the rules of logic;[71] or
   o because of the lack of mental resources[72]

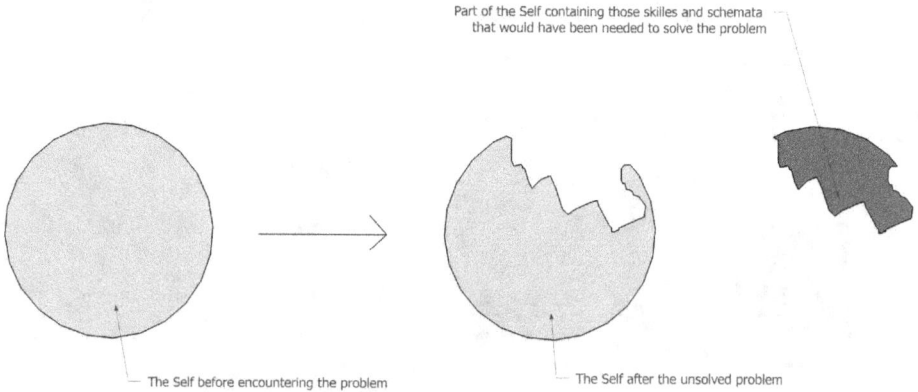

Part of the Self containing those skilles and schemata that would have been needed to solve the problem

The Self before encountering the problem

The Self after the unsolved problem

Figure 29: Losing a part of our Self due to failure

In case 1, there is a gap of several levels between the existing cognitive schemata

---

[67]   the way we structure our schemata, the way we solve problems
[68]   how quickly we manipulate the schemata
[69]   which has to be overcome in order to divide the schema into parts
[70]   for example, for a three-year-old child, 543+675 = ?
[71]   for example, think of a number which is smaller than five but bigger than 7
[72]   for example, multiply 876,231 by 982,312 in your head

and those required for the solution.[73] In everyday life, this may be the most frustrating type of problem (followed by the greatest Self-narrowing), since it can be perceived that the solution exists, only that our schemata are not good enough. If our schemata are inadequate, it means that we cannot model a certain part of the Environment, and are then confronted with the borders of our Selves.

This may create a division or reduction of the Self, forcing us to reassess our borders and restructure our Selves. This happens at a much increased rate if it requires an ability we thought we had.

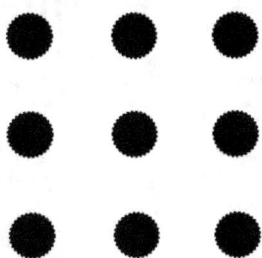

Figure 30: Brainteaser: try to connect the 9 points with a single line that passes through the all of the points and changes course only 3 times

The second type is not a real problem, as it has a solution: namely, that it is a contradiction in terms, at least within those frameworks we accept, it contradicts certain basic statements. In this case, it is the uncertainty that troubles us, as it raises the question whether there could be a way to modify the frameworks[74] in such a way that this problem also has a solution. Namely, that everyone has already experienced that new event, or feeling, which can only be established when we change the paradigm.[75]

However, the third type relates to the question of mental capacity: our memory is not endless, so the number of cognitive schemata we can manipulate at any one time is limited. Everything beyond this limit is unmanageable, or can be managed only very slowly and with different auxiliary techniques. For example, we can use our fingers to solve the abovementioned problem, or imagine it in a written form etc.. If the problem requires far more capacity, or cannot be solved, does not cause so much frustration, as the solution is 'the capacity of my brain does not allow me to answer'.

---

[73] staying with the example: the concepts of numbers, summation, digits et al
[74] technically, paradigms
[75] cf. out-of-the-box-thinking, when one can step out of the frameworks and is able to look at the problem from a higher level, thus bringing new solutions

SELF   ENVIRONMENT

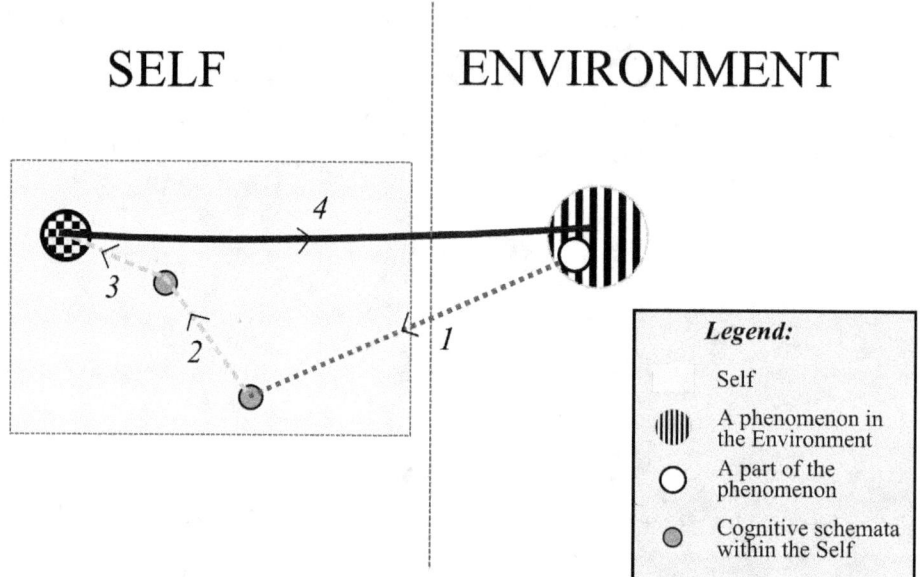

A part of a phenomenon activates (1) a cognitive schema within the Self. This schema activates (2, 3) others until the schema representing the whole phenomena is activated (4)

Figure 31: The process of finding an extant solution

Finding Extant Solutions

The simplest case is when the solution of the problem is readily available. Amongst the person's cognitive schemata there may be one which properly represents the Environment. The only issue is of recalling this schema. Most often this happens through several metastases: the person identifies a detail of the problem which he can recall, the connecting schemata then activate, which finally[76] activates the schema representing the solution of the problem fully and properly.

For example, when we do not see a whole apple, only a part of it upon which we see the apple's seeds as well. The seeds activate the schema of the apple's core, which activate the schema of the apple.

Figure 32: We recognize an image based on just a part of it (apple)

---

[76]   possibly by connecting with other schemata

Establishing a new schema

Establishing a new schema is unlike drawing on blank paper. No schema can remain unconnected within the Self, as it would then never be activated for lack of a link to it; every new schema should be built on the old/previous schemata. The old schemata cannot fall into pieces and restructure itself or themselves, as they have the parts that preserve the internal relationships of those pieces. These relationships connect the old and new to other, pre-existing, schemata.

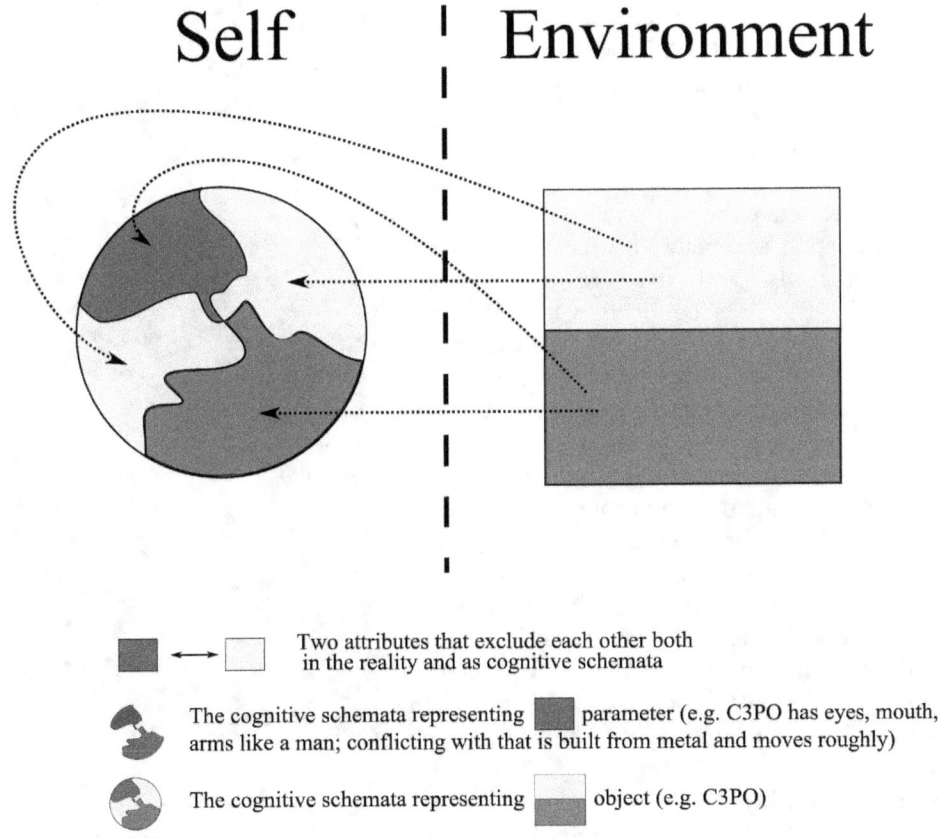

Two attributes that exclude each other both in the reality and as cognitive schemata

The cognitive schemata representing ▮ parameter (e.g. C3PO has eyes, mouth, arms like a man; conflicting with that is built from metal and moves roughly)

The cognitive schemata representing ▭ object (e.g. C3PO)

Figure 33: Two conflicting parts of the same object, and the activated schemata

As described in 'The manipulation of partial-schemata', a schema can fall into pieces rebuild itself, and so a new schema is established. This occurs when certain elements of the old schema do not represent the Environment proper, as there is no agreement between the two parts of it, one or both of them is/are wrong. The same situation occurs when two separate schema do not fit each other, despite both of them partially describing the Environment.

The Self tries to declare one of the competing ones unusable, and attempts to convince itself that that one is irrelevant on this occasion. If the Self can convince itself to neglect one, it would then be free to use the other competing schema. To achieve this, the Self activates increasingly deeper levels of sub-schemata within the two competing schemata.

For example, on the attached figure the viewer cannot decide whether he sees a man or a machine. It is made of metal, but it has eyes and hands. It has no skin, but its head and extremities are discernible, and so on. This man or machine conflict maintains until he – it – realizes that it is an android. If he could reject the possibility that it is a man, then he would have considered it as a machine, which would then raise the questions of what this machine is for, how it functions etc.

The more active the sub-schemata beneath the two competing schemata are, the more intense the conflict is, and the greater the Self-narrowing. But the connection of the sub-schemata can dissolve just as they are established, and can be reshaped within a new group. These attempts at connection are termed problem solving. The new schema is established when the partial schemata – by bridging the differences – may form a new group that integrates everything by different connections within and between the schemata. The establishment of the new schema does not cancel the opposition between the former two schemata,[77] but integrates them in a new way. The better the integration of the two schemata,[78] and the more unambiguous it is internally,[79] the more stable and usable it is.

A certain quality assurance is obtained if the brain keeps the number of contradictory connections below an acceptable minimum.[80] As with quality controls in manufacturing, after a test phase it can be stated that a new 'product'

Figure 34: Is this a man, or a machine? (Android called 'C-3PO' from the movie Star Wars)

---

[77] so the concept of the android does not confuse the terms of man and machine
[78] the more parts (elements, partial schemata) are successfully integrated
[79] so that there are no contradictions between the partial schemata
[80] this 'acceptance level' differs from person to person, and is viewed as demand level. When we say that 'somebody has high standards', we mean that his acceptance level is high; he cannot accept too many contradictory connections

has been made : the new cognitive schema. This also demonstrates that it does not matter if we have some intuition about the right method. We check the principal

points before becoming suffi-ciently satisfied to share it with our social environment. The main role of the social Envi-ronment, besides using the new schema, is that it is a part of the testing process: when we tell our friends a new idea or solution, they – with good or bad intentions – will criticize it, so trying to assist us in making an unambiguous cognitive schema.

Testing is nothing other than applying the new schema to different situations, facts etc. As it is nothing other than es-tablishing newer connections with existing schemata, thus it offers increasingly higher level integration with the set of cognitive schemata. Until this testing brings positive results, by making more and more positive connections to the cognitive schema,[81] the Self expands more and more. This Self-expansion acts as a posi-tive affirmation (to an optimal level), and the cognitive schema

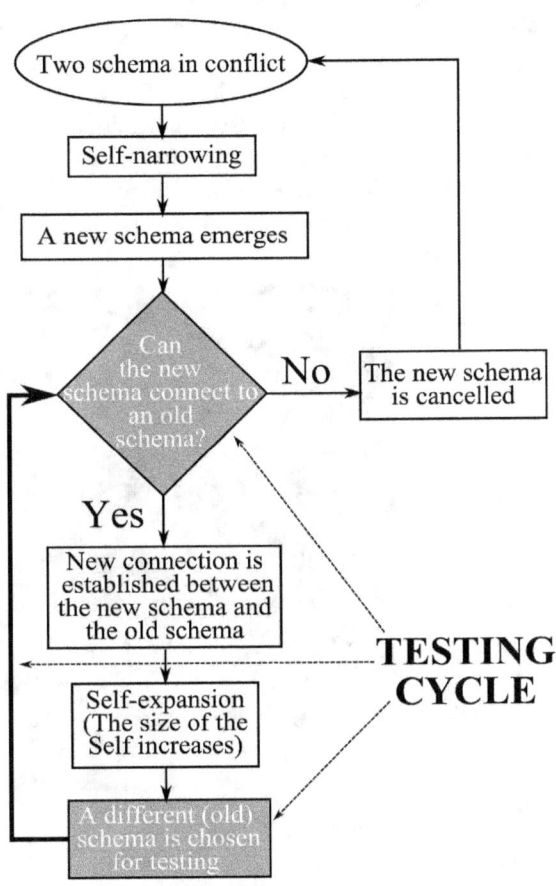

Figure 35: - The process of testing

urges the person to further sharing and testing.

Behind the Self-expansion, the more connections the new schema makes, the more often it provides a more valuable answer[82] than those previous, and so in-creases the power of the Self over the Environment; or, equally, it decreases the Self's defenselessness in the face of the Environment. This is achieved as, by being able to model the Environment, it can be manipulated or dealt with in a manner that could not be done before.

---

[81] in the mind of the person and that of the social Environment
[82] more usable, more precise, faster

Self-narrowing is bound to a tendency to do away with one of the two competing schemata in order to be free to use the other; this tendency leads to a certain type of aggression. The aggression is rooted in the mental effort required to disable those connections that activated the cognitive schema, and which are to be ignored; this requires intense concentration. For example, to ignore the possibility that there is a man in the picture above, having decided that we want to see it as a machine. Aggression is also an adequate answer, as until the Self can no longer model the Environment properly, it is in danger: since the model is wrong the Environment is less manageable, its reaction or behavior cannot be predicted, and such Environments threaten the existence of the Self.[83]

Figure 36: Tomato with an outgrowth

In many cases, the appearance of aggression solves the problem. Think of a tomato that we want to give to someone as a gift, but upon it is an outgrowth, a smaller tomato. By breaking off the small tomato (which in our example is the appearance of aggression) we obtain a 'perfect' tomato, and can now give it to the target person.

If we look more closely at the example, we notice a small misinterpretation within it. By breaking the small part off, we obtain a nice tomato. However, the small one will have left a mark upon it. This is the beauty of the example: it shows that aggression does not lead to a perfect solution, as two things were connected, and we removed one of the two competing schema (the small tomato) in vain; the trace of the former link indicates that this is no longer a whole, only a part of the whole. Perhaps expansion of the example is a trifle forced, but maybe the best

[83] To expand this example, let us imagine that we are in an examination, and our result depends upon describing exactly what C3PO is

solution is if we give the juice of both the big and small tomato to the target person, thus preserving the original whole, as in tomato juice the two ingredients do not divide. Of course, the connection between the shape and the content of the tomato has been dissolved again, by squeezing. This is considered to be an aggressive act, as the trace of the missing link will be visible again.

A small detour: the missing link always indicates that it is not the whole, and that it is in a state preceded by aggression: it is not accidental that people shy from the sight of a truncated body, even if it is not bloody or the wound is not fresh. The trace of the link –, for example, the site of the missing limb – indicates the preceding aggression and the injury of the whole, thus it cannot activate a whole schema. That is why it can be difficult for us to perceive an injured person as physically whole.

Satisfying the hunger for problems

The abovementioned connection, according to which Self-expansion has a positive reinforcing effect, has further consequences. Those people for whom problem solving causes more Self-expansion than Self-narrowing, will seek further possibilities for Self-expansion through searching out problems and solving them.

But when does problem solving in general provide one with more Self-expansion than Self-narrowing? This happens when:

o he can solve the problems he faces because of his abilities
o he faces problems which fit his abilities
o his social Environment is suitable for sharing his newly-established schemata, and thus he gains further Self-expansion.

To make the above list more understandable, let us examine a few examples from the world of children and school:

Maybe it is easiest to admit that a very intelligent, creative child, with a good memory, has a greater ability to solve problems than his schoolmates of poorer ability. He experiences Self-expansion more often, and will enjoy meeting problems, since he has a bigger chance of solving them than failing and, in doing so, obtain Self-expansion.

The proper choice of a problem's level of difficulty can help any child to come to enjoy challenges. Even with lesser abilities, if a teacher gives him problems which accord with his intellectual level, knowledge and main abilities – for example, visual creativity, fine motor function,[84] technical sense, physical abilities etc. – then his sense of competence, and his Self, will grow, and he will with pleasure seek future challenges. The opposite of this is also true. If the child with greater abilities faces overly simple tasks, then the Self-narrowed periods will be short (as he solves the problems easily) and, as a result, the Self-expansion cannot be that important either. So he loses interest in solving problems as a "source of Self-

---

[84]   namely, manual skills

expansion", and will look for other sources; sport, sex, drugs, gambling etc. That leads his Self through bigger Self-narrowing/Self-expansion phases. We can go further: standards set too high can cause proportionately greater Self-narrowing, even in children with good abilities, which also diverts them from seeking out problems.[85]

We already know that family background determines a child's performance in school, regardless of their mental abilities. This can be considered more generally. The social Environment with which the child shares his schemata was originally defined as absolutely subjective, so not necessarily the parents or the teacher have to be the important people with whom the child shares his pleasure arising from the new schemata; it could be an old neighbor, or a distant relative. In spite of this, the class, teachers and parents usually offer a determining pattern on sharing knowledge. They provide an atmosphere allowing the child to increase the pleasure that comes from the Self-expansion following problem solving. The best example of the opposite situation is an unhealthy atmosphere in a class. Here, lack of preparation and knowledge, coupled with foolishness, come into play; for example, because a child of weak mental ability becomes the central character. Such an atmosphere does not aid problem solving, or sharing that with others. It limits the circle of friends who can function as a social Environment. Moreover, the child cannot have Self-expansion on their own undisturbed, as they will be at a disadvantage if friends catch sight of it. The same applies within the family. The child may discover the parents as partners[86] with whom to share the new schemata discovered at school. The child can tell them, and the parents may even understand what new things he realized in class, and further contribute to the child's ability to both seek problems and to share the joy of the solutions at home.

To summarize…The fortunate concurrence of the abovementioned circumstances, which I consider as a task for teachers and parents, provides a type of hunger for established problems. This prompts young people to apprehend, throughout their lives, that part of life which is more difficult, but also provides more pleasure. This hunger for problems is a key issue for, inter alia, successful careers in many fields.

Natural – and artificial – self-confidence (narcissism)

The majority of parents realize, after evaluating their own – and others – careers, that if they want to see their child become a successful person, then that hunger for problems and knowledge must appear in the child. Many people go further, and say that the greater the hunger for problems, the greater the success the child will achieve. This statement also applies to the first approach. Although a different

---

[85]   this is similar to the phenomenon of "learned helplessness", when people learn that they cannot change anything in their lives. Their Selves shrink artificially and disproportionately to their abilities, and after a while they give up trying to make their lives better. They do not feel that they can affect their Environment, and are always filled with anguish because of their exposure to the Environment

[86]   so that the parents can function as his social Environment

issue, whatever sacrifice success may require,[87] for most of the parents[88] no thought is given to this.

In order to proceed, let us accept the following hypothesis as true of parents: "the greater the hunger for problems, the more successful the child". Note that this assumption incorrectly emphasizes something other than happiness; it is not saying "the greater the hunger for problems, the greater the Self-expansion," and these Self-expansions will lead to a happy life.

Unfortunately,[89] parents have the power to artificially intervene and so increase the appetite for problems. How are such interventions made?

False feedback: constant compliments – such as how skillful/clever/nice you are – can increase the Self-expansion of the child after successful problem solving. This may result in a happy child in the short term, and have a reinforcing effect in that the child seeks out new problems and, by solving these, satisfy his and his environment's need for success

The child is given seemingly difficult, but actually easy, tasks. In this case he does not obtain greater Self-expansion than he deserves, as the Self-narrowing was not that great. However, the proportions of Self-expansion (after establishing a new cognitive schema) and Self-expansion (after sharing this schema) will be permanently distorted. This creates and builds a strong dependence on social Environment in the long term, as he will expect Self-expansion later in his life, not so much from actual performance, but from social approval, partners, family and friends.

Where does this artificial inflation of the Self, and constant seeking of Self-expansion, eventually lead?

One possibility previously mentioned is when the performance, due to greater ability, is outstanding, but the hunger for problems can never be satisfied. So, a burden of performance emerges, which relies only on one source of Self-expansion: problem solving by using the intellect. This disturbs the balance of the personality, that which comes from the possibility to obtain Self-expansion from different sources, such as via human relations, physical activities etc.[90]

It can lead to cheating. When the apparent activity that causes further Self-expansion ends, then the Self-expansion, coming from a disproportionate reflection, can only be reached by artificial tools that provide disproportionate effects; for example, through drugs or criminal activity. The problem with these is that they cause substantial Self-expansion only in the short term. In the long term, its negative consequences stand out: it might be good to rob banks, as a lot of money is obtained quickly. In the longer term, however, he is pursued by police. Constantly hiding from them causes anxiety which leads to Self-narrowing.

If there is artificial inflation, there can also be eruption. When a person realizes

---

[87]   health, mental balance, human relations etc.

[88]   especially those who were unsuccessful, and are now compensating for this at the cost of their children

[89]   it would be better if the parents could forget their own goals and competitive attitudes, and focus mostly on their children's happiness, rather than on their performance

[90]   cf. Enlightenment section on specialists in a narrow subject with no other interest

that some people[91] lied to him, that is hurtful, especially if these people are close relatives, who provide the frame of reference in many fields of life. This fracture in somebody's life causes greater Self-narrowing, although this may still be the 'least worst' scenario compared with the two alternatives mentioned above.[92]

A person with an artificially inflated Self may find it difficult to realize that they in that condition. Even if – as a result of a personal tragedy or a serious interpersonal problem[93] – they did realize this, to rectify that would be extremely painful for them. No one is happy about giving up the status he has reached, especially when he is used to fighting for everything and ceding nothing. This lies behind the condition called narcissism. Narcissism[94] goes with an overly high level of aspiration, and thus an incapability of achieving happiness, which may cause other mental diseases or problems.

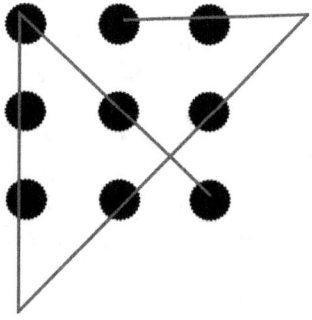

Figure 37: Solution of the nine points problem

A good example of solving a problem is by reinterpreting these frames: who said that you are not allowed to leave the imaginary square around the dots?

Principal points covered in this chapter:
- selecting and using cognitive schemata
- determining whether problems are capable of being solved
- Self-confidence and narcissism

---

[91]   even with good intentions
[92]   being a specialist in a narrow subject with no other interest or cheating
[93]   for example, losing their job, or a divorce
[94]   self-love

7. UNDERSTANDING AGGRESSION BY DEFINING DIFFERENT TYPES OF RELATIONSHIPS

Objects, entities, and their see-saw relationships. * A schema as absolute ruler. * Separating or compressing models; strength or weakness? * Magnetic attraction…or repulsion? * Connections; the energy they require, and mixed messages. * Classical and FIPP concepts of aggression. * Aggression can narrow the Self. * But does it look like that? * Intimidation of groups. * Aggression can be good for you. * Verbal versus physical violence: the decider?

Introduction: the types of relationships between objects

Before examining the concept of aggression, let us examine more closely how we define something, and which possible relationships two cognitive schemata can have.

How does a definition work?

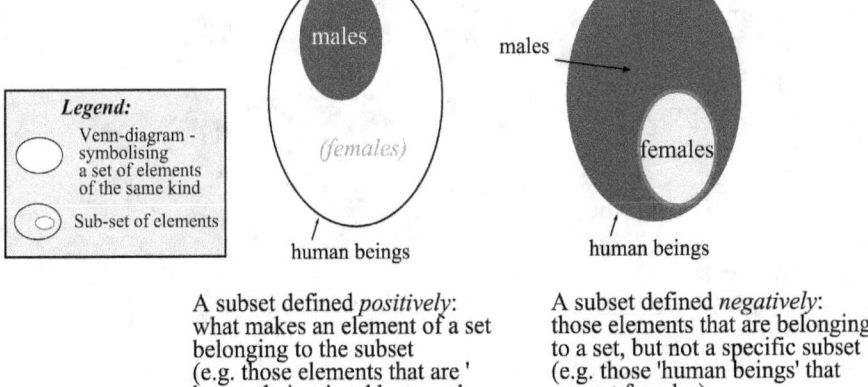

A subset defined *positively*: what makes an element of a set belonging to the subset (e.g. those elements that are 'human beings' and have male sexual organs)

A subset defined *negatively*: those elements that are belonging to a set, but not a specific subset (e.g. those 'human beings' that are not females)

Figure 38: Defining 'man' in two ways

When we would like to define something (for example, what is a man?), there are two ways to do that:

o in a positive way: we specify what it is (a man is a human being with masculine sexual organs) OR

o in a negative way: we specify what it is not (a human being that is not a woman)

Note:

o when we define in a positive way, we do not obtain further information on other things that might belong to the same group (in our case, there is no information on women)

o when we define in a negative way, we have to know exactly the definition of those entities that were excluded

o the negative way is not that precise, as there might be other members of the set that are not taken into consideration (for example, the hermaphrodites in our case are also taken as men).

Relationships between two entities

As numbers and logic fundamentally determine both our thinking and our view of the world, the truth of mathematics also affects how we look at – amongst other things – relationships. A simple form of this is to describe the relationship between different entities[95] as positive,[96] neutral (nil) or negative.[97] This describes the implicit manner in which two entities affect each other during their relationship. However, until we define and measure the effect precisely – not only its direction – we are satisfied with knowing that:

o they help each other's activity (for example, when neurons stimulate each other); or

o they hold each other up (for example, when neurons inhibit each other); and

o the condition in which they have nothing to do with each other, maintains, so that the entities are independent.[98]

Let us define the relationship between cognitive schemata along analogous lines, but with a small dif-

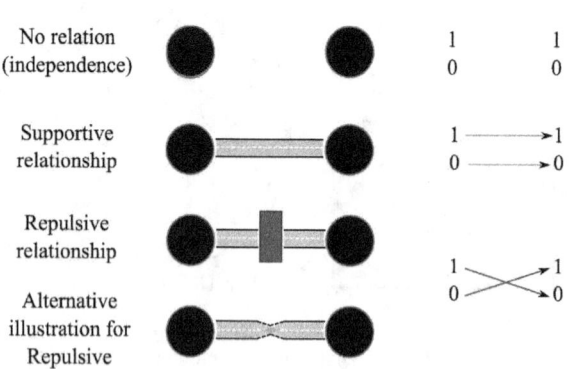

Figure 39: Basic relationship types

---

ference, by dividing the three connections into two differing subtypes:
- o where there is a connection between them (as when there is a road between two cities); and
- o where there is no connection between them (as when there is no road between two cities).

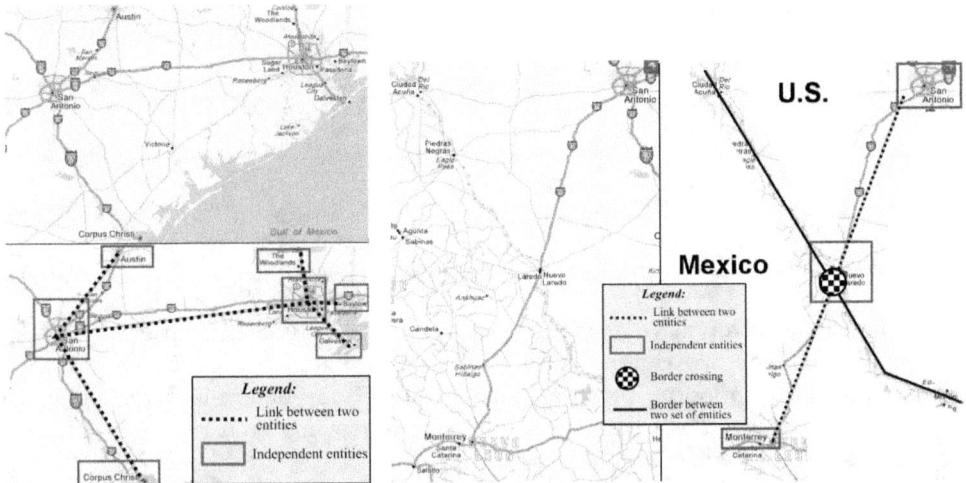

Figure 41: Supportive relationship   Figure 40: Repulsive relationship

When there is a connection between them, then:
- o either information streams through it (as when we are free to travel between cities). Let us call this a supportive relationship;
- o or the streaming of information is forbidden.[99] Let us call this a repulsive relationship. A good way of imagining a repulsive relationship is when we try to define something not by what it is, but by what it is not.[100]

What is the consequence of these defined relationships? In the case of supportive connections, the information streams between the connected schemata so freely, and quickly, that it is almost impossible from an external viewpoint to distinguish the individual elements from either each other or the whole. On the contrary, repulsive connections actively separate whole schemata from each other, thus limiting what is a part of one and what is not.

---

[99] when in the middle of the road between two cities/countries armed guards make sure nobody passes through; the Iron Curtain, the Berlin Wall

[100] for example, we do not say John is a man, rather that John is not a woman

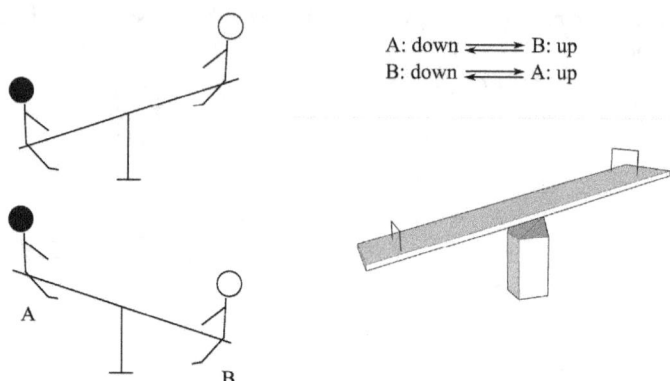

Figure 42: See-saw

To illustrate the repulsive relationship using visual analogy, let us use the see-saw (teeter-totter). The two children sitting on a see-saw are connected to each other, but always in an opposite position. One position fully determines the other. In mathematical terms, the relationship is A=not(B), so that if A changes, B has to change as well, and vice versa.

Such divisions of relationships, especially the "merging" effect of supportive connections, explain how it is possible that lower-level schemata and their integrations (the higher-level schemata) are at once different and yet the same.

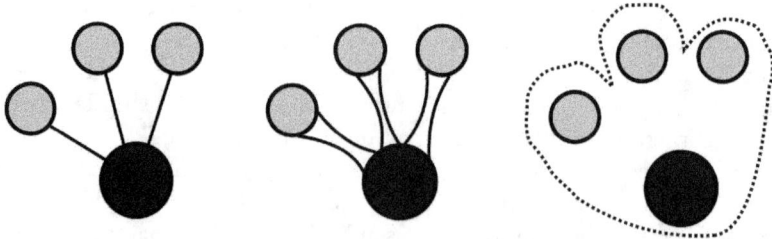

Figure 43: Different ways of illustrating a schema and its 'children' schemata

Why are these connections interesting in the case of aggression? That is what we shall now look at.

Perceiving the Environment exclusively by a sole schema representative of it

Establishment of the absolute ruler schema by integration

As seen in the descriptions of FIPP[101] and function practice,[102] the relationship of the Environment and the Self is fundamentally determined by how successfully we can represent the surrounding world with models called cognitive schemata. A person dominates his Environment when the schemata used at a particular moment is, alone, capable of gathering and processing, without contradiction, information in connection with the relevant events, objects and phenomena of the world.

We can define the final goal of all problem solving as the Self representing the Environment as a single unambiguous schema (having only supportive connections within it). One way of achieving this goal was described in Problem Solving: mismatched schemata represent different parts and aspects of the Environment, out of which a new schema emerges, which then represents the former two (or more) schemata in an unambiguous way. The Environment is then modeled as an absolute ruler schema.

Other methods of establishing the absolute ruler schema

That two (or more) schemata do not match is caused by repulsive connections between them. To dissolve such connections, there can be integration with restructuring. In addition, there are two other procedures that lead to a representation in the form of a schema. It is characteristic of both that they reverse the connections that play a role in the non-matching, in order to rid themselves of contradictions. The two solutions are

o separation; and
o compression.

Separation occurs when a supporting connection ends as it connects to a part that makes the schema contradictory. A gruesome illustration occurs in those countries where the hands of thieves are cut off as punishment. Another example is where a region of a country separates, declaring independence from its motherland.

In compression, repulsive connections are turned into supportive ones. So, those parts originally separated become connected; for example, when we try to put two non-matching puzzle pieces together by force. However, to add another grisly example, a knife – something which does not fit with a body naturally – is pushed into somebody. Alternatively, where a country is invaded and forcibly subsumed into the territory of the invading country against the will of its citizens.

---

[101] see Chapter 3
[102] see Chapter 12

The characteristics of separation and compression

By considering the abovementioned examples and descriptions, reversing the connections (making a supportive one out of a repulsive one, and vice versa), mostly leads to a socially less valuable output than the initial state. However, separation and compression as such are cognitive processes that of themselves do not have value: they simply improve or weaken the model of their Environment. The common name for the two processes (supportive and repulsive) is aggression. It does not contradict the known psychological fact that there are socially valuable forms of aggression.[103]

That aggression – and within it separation – is a useful process, one easy to observe in the manipulation of schemata. We have seen in Problem Solving that, before establishing a new schema, we must first manipulate the pieces of certain schemata: we attempt systematically to put them together in order to find a new, better, fit. The separation of the partial schemata from each other plays a key role in this process. Note that, although it would seem logical to attribute the leading role to the process of separation, when the new schema is suddenly established from the many parts, it probably does not happen like this. The connections temporarily cease to be (as if there were never any connections) and the completely new schema is formed on the basis of its independence from each other. This also displays a difference between the technique of establishing a schema by complete reconstruction, and the technique of dividing them into parts and trying to fit them to each other randomly.

Another obvious advantage of separation is seen when the complete schema from which we separate something, has no relevance for the Self. For example, when a sculptor crafts a beautiful shape out of a large stone; although the shapeless stone is a schema, it is completely irrelevant for the Self of the person who observes the sculptor. This is the converse of the Self of the sculptor, who has to have a precise picture of where cracks and faults are, where the stone is hard or soft, where and in which direction it can be cleaved in order to shape it. A similar, less artistic example is a quarryman who strikes a stone. The only important thing for him is to make smaller pieces of stone; to divide a bigger whole into smaller parts.

Another example better demonstrates the aggressive nature of separation. If I pull a key out of a lock then push it back, nothing happens. However, if I break and then glue back together a porcelain vase, we realize that the distinction lies in the different cases of separation. For the "key-in-the-lock", the constituent parts have the schemata that represent themselves; the "key-in-the-lock" schema can integrate them. The pieces of the porcelain vase are not independent schemata, thus the compression (the gluing) is not a possible method of integration. Aggression in this case is akin to breaking the vase into pieces, which cannot be reinte-

---

[103]   for example, defense forces

grated.[104] Separation is exactly the same in both cases. The difference is whether it happens to two separate schemata that are in a repulsive relationship with each other.

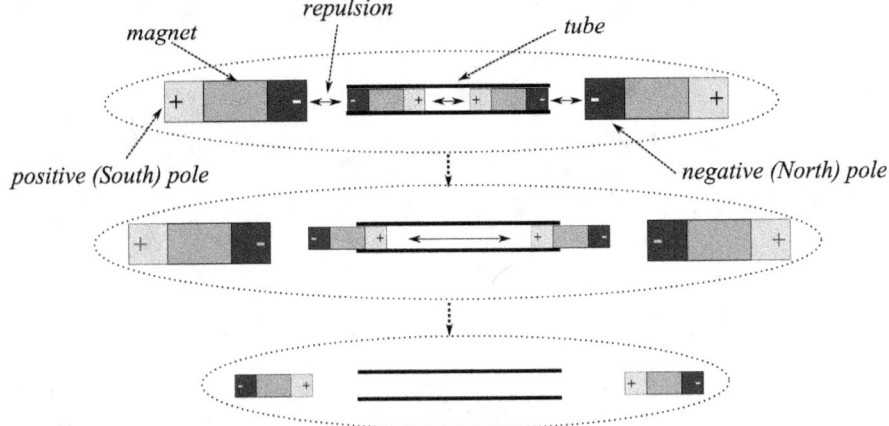

Figure 44: Magnetic attraction and repulsion

This position can be demonstrated with two magnets, the poles of which are aligned and so should repulse each other. Yet they do not move from each other as outer effects hold them together (two larger magnets, of higher strength, push them towards each other on the image). As soon as the outer effect ceases, the magnets move to a distance from each other where they no longer repel each other.[105] The repelling effect of the magnets is similar to repulsion, and the outer cohesive effect parallels the compression.

Mixed types of connections

The situation is different when not all the connections are repulsive, but there are supportive connections as well as repulsive ones (see image). In this case, only integration with restructuring can help to avoid mixing the connections.

Mixing of connections is also of key importance in compression. We can make stable connections, equal in value to connections based on integration, if no repulsive connections remain between the sub-schemata.[106]

---

[104] only if we purposefully do it
[105] according to the law of physics, to an infinite distance
[106] for example, when we have a cork and a bottle in our hands, we have two separate, distinct schemata. When we begin to cork the bottle, overcoming the friction between the cork and the mouth of the bottle, by overcoming the repulsive effects we establish supporting connections. The supporting connection in this example is the adhesion (friction) between the cork and the mouth of the bottle, which does not let the cork come out, even if there is increased pressure in the bottle. We have then established from this the "schema of corking"

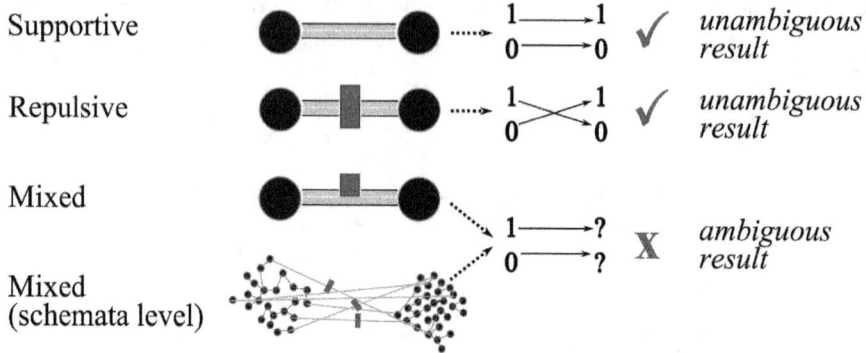

Figure 45: Ambiguous connections lead to uncertainty

To summarize, mixing supportive and repulsive connections generates an unstable situation due to the uncertainty that it leads to.[107] The uncertainty comes from the situation that, if an active schema is connected ambiguously to another schema, should that increase its activity, or would that decrease its activity level? That is why the aim is always to have either repulsive or supportive relations within both two schemata and their sub-schemata.

The energy of connections

In both separation and compression, establishing and modifying connections takes effort. For example, in chemistry, the connections between atoms are known as chemical bonds. Chemistry describes the concept of binding energy, that energy required to disassemble two – or more – connected atoms of a molecule.[108]

Staying with chemistry, we are able to measure precisely and examine the energy used in separation and compression. In mental processes, we can, at best, indicate only the types of relationships (increasing, decreasing, bigger, smaller) during the processes, as they are difficult to measure. It is almost certain that the energy used in the mental processes has nothing to do with the energy surrounding what is happening in reality. The energy required to activate an atomic bomb by pushing a button has no association with the energy released on the explosion. Also, there is no connection between the physical and mental energy required for the extraction and carving of stone. It seems most likely that it is the number of connections to

---

[107] similar to the situation when we press on a car's accelerator and brake at the same time. How should the car react?

[108] example: in order to disassemble the H_2O water molecule to an O atoms and two H atoms, we have to place an electric current through the water via an anode and a cathode. The energy (electricity) is required to dissolve the hydrogen-oxygen connections in the water molecules. To make two atoms join (at least initially) also requires energy (during the joining process the same amount of energy is generated as is needed to dissolve them). Usually, this generated energy feeds the process after it has begun: when we light a fire we provide the energy needed for starting, then the process sustains itself

be changed that most determines the mental energy: the more sub-schemata connected to a sub-schema, the greater the energy required. It is important to note that the one significance of the level of a schema is that a higher-level schema has more sub-schemata, and can thus have more connections; the sub-schemata of lower-level schemata have fewer bonds.

Note that, if we could ensure that the cognitive schemata operate in accordance with general systems theory, further examination of this bonding energy, and of the energy flows of a system, might provide interesting results.

Another important question in changing the connections is the relationship of the schemata and the Environment. Mentally, we can only deal with schemata and their related connections. However, the schemata represent the Environment. Until the Environment changes,[109] there will be discrepancies (contradictions) between what we perceive and the schemata we have. Accordingly, we either modify our schemata so that they model the Environment,[110] or we modify the Environment to make it accept our schemata.[111] The third option is to try to avoid realizing such differences between the Environment and our schemata.[112] This third alternative is the least attractive, as it does not provide a real solution, and eventually the Environment behaves in a manner difficult to overcome on a cognitive level.[113] Regardless of this, this solution is widely used, as it often requires less energy than do the two 'modifying' solutions.

Separation and compression as Self-narrowing effects

The establishment of the schemata means a positive confirmation for the Self.[114] At the same time, modification of the connections is not Self-narrowing if a higher-level order can only be made by switching the connections. This requires consistent connections (either only supporting or only repulsive, but not mixed) between two schemata, or not to have contradictory schemata.

Inconsistency can be illustrated visually with images in which there are holes in the wall (supportive relationships amongst repulsive ones), or when there are potholes on the road (a few repulsive ones among supportive relationships). Such inconsistencies remaining within a schema do not provide obvious answers if we want to use the schema. It is only a matter of time before the contradictions emerge as problems.

Nevertheless, if we have too many inconsistent schemata it narrows the Self, as with the problem, so we can state that separation and compression cause Self-

---

109 through our actions or activity, or independent of us

110 this is called passive adaptation; an example is how we think about the relationship of the Earth and the stars, whether the Earth goes around them etc.

111 this is so-called active adaptation, as when we excavate passes through mountains to build railways or highways

112 for example, when we do not want to notice that raindrops are falling because we want to barbecue outside

113 for example, it begins to rain so much that it puts out the barbecue fire

114 as it has more and more tools to represent the Environment so that it can exert an increasingly greater effect on the outer world, becomes increasingly safer, and thus has a Self-expansion effect

narrowing. The greater the number and size of the inconsistencies,[115] the more Self-narrowing is caused.

The aggression concept of FIPP, and classic psychology

In psychology, there are different groups of aggression according to the aim (for example, self-defense, territorial acquisition), the method (verbal, physical) and the form (latent, mental, auto-aggression) of aggressive behavior. Despite our feeling that there is something common in these manifestations of aggression (which is why we talk about the same concept), defining it properly, and including all the forms of it in the meantime, is difficult. The difficulty of the definition arises principally from the duality of behavioral manifestation and mental processes; someone can say something nice about us and yet wish us in hell at the same time. Or he gives us his knife with the hope that we will cut ourselves with it. The difference in behavior/mental process is more clearly seen in passive aggression, when we do something by doing nothing. It is the negligence of an altruistic act.[116]

The aggression concept of FIPP

When we first examined FIPP, we admitted that Environment is a completely subjective construct. Thus, we could clearly demonstrate both the priority of mental processes and that the change of the Environment is merely a result of the changes of our schemata. Such separation of the outside world and a person's Self, while emphasizing mental functions, explains amongst other things the equality of word, thought, negligence and act preached by different religions. As everything (talking, inaction and movement) is represented on the level of schemata, thus from his psyche's point of view it is practically all the same. This is the case no matter whether the child merely has detailed daydreams about hitting his younger brother, or actually does so.

In harmony with the above, FIPP defines aggression as follows: aggression is nothing other than separation and compression performed on the level of cognitive schemata (independent of whether it will appear in any form of change in the outside world).

Verifying FIPP's definition of aggression in relation to the results of psychology to date

To verify whether this definition – which appears elegant at first – is in harmony with the current state of psychology, and whether it explains the former connections that have a paradigmatic effect, let us examine the so-called frustration-aggression theory. According to this theory, manifestations of aggression are pre-

---

[115]   so that the proportion of the repulsive and supportive connections between two schemata is 50-50, instead of five or six connections of the schemata connecting with, say, 2,000-3,000 contradictory connections

[116]   for example, not holding out our arm to prevent somebody about to walk off a pavement into traffic

ceded by frustration in the majority of cases. Accordingly, people respond with either regression[117] or aggression when they are frustrated. But what is frustration? Psychology defines it as a hindrance in reaching a goal. According to FIPP, this is nothing other than the simultaneous presence of two mismatching schemata (one is the attractive goal, the other the obstacle itself).

Rarely do we have the possibility – or time – to integrate the schema of the aim and the schema of the obstacle, so separating the obstacle and the connected aim, then dividing it into parts hoping that with the pieces it will not connect to the schema of the aim. For example, we break the door, since the wooden pieces of the door cannot prevent us from entering the house. If the disintegrated schema was irrelevant for the Self in the first place (so that it is not connected to anything), then aggression is a solution. Nevertheless – staying with the former example – if we built the door with our own hands and are proud of it, breaking it is not such a good solution.

The relationship of aggression and Self-narrowing

We have seen from the former descriptions that a problem can have different solutions.[118] It can be solved with integration, when there will be one schema out of two schemata, but we can also detach one of them and 'terminate' it by slicing it into pieces. The question remains, which one to use?

To answer that, we have to understand that Self-narrowing is caused not only by aggression, but also that Self-narrowing leads to aggression. This happens during Self-narrowing and manipulating schemata; series of separations and compressions occur as a pot-luck method of problem solving.

We could say that the strategy chosen depends upon our personality. But we can go further: if we destroy one of the competing schemata, we recognize and record x amount of Self-narrowing. If we wait until we find the schema (the solution with integration), during the search process we will also have Self-narrowing, the most extreme value of which would be y. The difference between them is that x remains even after solving the problem, while y turns to z Self-expansion, where z is proportionate to y. But we have an amount of uncertainty as to whether our Self-narrowing will turn into the same amount of Self-expansion as a result of finding the integrative solution.

If our former experience shows that[119] we often find the integrative solution, then we will undergo y Self-narrowing, because it will be compensated for, and the solution will be stable. If we do not trust our abilities then it is easier for us to live with x Self-narrowing, and we will choose the disintegrative solution.

According to this, our persistence in trying to find the long-term solution depends upon the following:

o the relationship of x and y (which one is larger)

---

[117] returning to a former stage of personality development

[118] solution of a problem: making a new schema out of two non-matching schemata

[119] due to our skills

o our experience of how often we find the solution for these kinds of questions
(how high is our pyramid of schemata of the field under discussion)
o our ability to bear y Self-narrowing

The relationship of x and y is provided by the situation. Our former experiences
and abilities come from self-knowledge. And the last, the ability to bear Self-
narrowing, is explained in psychology by the concept of frustration tolerance.

The second point (experience) is determined not only by confidence but also by
our tendency to take risks (how risk-averse we are). Other aspects are: the time we
have (although finding the solution during the time we have counts in deliberating
our chances, and shows a connection with how fast we usually are in finding solutions); and, our general condition (for example, hormonal condition) which influences the decision as well.

At the same time, there are those who have positive experiences with disintegrative solutions; for example, because they are generally in a more Self-narrowed
state.[120] For them, x Self-narrowing has a relatively smaller effect, which also passes
faster. So, they will more often choose a solution other than the integrative one.[121]

In accord with the foregoing, we can form a more precise picture of which solution we choose compared with simply predicting somebody's strategy of problem solving based only on personality characteristics. Also of importance is that
FIPP is both capable of handling the circumstances – the past, the present condition, and the problem, at the same time – and of reducing them to a common denominator.

The effect of the fluctuation of Self-narrowing on the appearance of aggression

In the previous sub-section, we referred briefly to the role of the general condition
in the appearance of aggression. Here, consider cases such as a yogi and an anxious, stressed-out yuppie stuck in traffic jams. Briefly disregard that they interpret
the situation differently, and assume that their position has an equally unpleasant
effect upon them. In the momentary Self-narrowing, the yuppie feels increasingly
disposed to behave aggressively; for example, he might overtake in the bus lane to
reach his aim, for which he gets a penalty for using the bus lane. Compare this
with the yogi, whose Self will also narrow, but will not reach the level which would
cause aggressive behavior to be exerted. He waits regardless that he will be late.

What happens if the yuppie practices yoga, so that these two people are the
same, only that his state of mind differs at two separate times? Their conditions
are determined primarily by the events of the previous hours,[122] their hormone
levels, and their health. A more efficient strategy might be where the previously
mentioned effects do not vanish in us without trace, but determine their actual
level of Self-narrowing as a random number generator. In other words, it is evolu-

---

[120] they may generally be anxious or aggressive
[121] people who are generally aggressive will tend to use aggressive solutions more often
[122] the Self-expansion and Self-narrowing of those hours

tionarily beneficial if the level of Self-narrowing is not constant, but constantly fluctuates. Why? Because there are sub-optimal[123] conditions of balance, and to turn away from these conditions we have to modify our general behavior: sometimes we may have to act as a yogi, sometimes as a yuppie. This conclusion is based on the mixed strategy described by game theory, which in most cases achieves a better result than the clean strategies. An example of a clean strategy is if my behavior is always based upon the same logic.[124] A mixed strategy is when, by leaving it to chance, we mix two or more clean strategies in certain proportions.[125] It is mathematically verifiable that mixed strategies generally lead to better results than clean strategies, even if they are obviously worse in one or two series.[126]

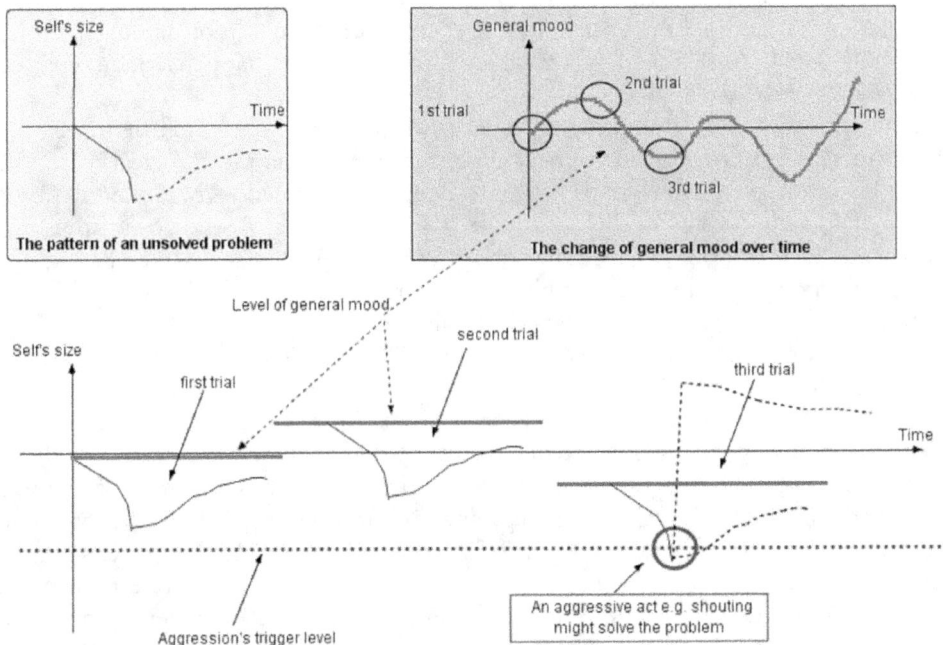

Figure 46: Solving a problem with aggression after several trials

From another viewpoint, the following can be stated: a fluctuating measure of Self acts as a generator of random factors needed to reach a mixed strategy.[127]

123 worse than the optimal, but still good
124 for example, whenever I bargain I initially offer how much I am prepared to pay; another strategy is to always wait for the seller to state the price
125 so before starting to bargain I flip a coin: if it is heads I declare my price first, if it is tails I wait for the seller to set the initial price
126 for example, by always obtaining heads, I might never obtain the lower prices I might otherwise expect from the seller, and vice versa
127 to use a mixed strategy requires random input. The fluctuating measure of the Self, similar to the flipping of

Based on all of this, in real life, sometimes quiet people have to make a stand, while vociferous people might occasionally find it worthwhile to restrain themselves.

Aggression and optimal group decision

The mixed strategy mentioned above also leads to positive results in group decisions. Recall Churchill's famous aphorism: "democracy is the worst form of government, except [for] all those other forms that have been tried from time to time". One interpretation of its meaning is that the opinion of the non-professional masses often pushes into the background those useful opinions that bring good solutions. Often, it is a problem in itself that certain solutions to a problem with multiple outcomes do not even enter the common knowledge or a debate, as they are so much against the mainstream. This happens at the cost of the group's creativity.

Another example from politics: a state is short of money,[128] and at first everyone urges increasing taxes, which seems logical. This logic is simple and clear to all: the state has money from taxes; if the state does not have enough money it needs more; if more money is needed, the state has to raise taxes. If we do not presume that taxes have an optimal level, then the government will raise taxes endlessly, disregarding the connection that the higher taxes imply, such as more people trying to avoid paying them by sending their money abroad.

So, the governing party urges the raising of taxes. Then somebody appears[129] and suggests that taxes be reduced.

In typical cases, others do not listen to him. Moreover, they accuse him of demagogy and populism. However, lower taxes attract more investors from abroad, people begin to invest their money in the country again instead of sending it abroad, and so on. Using this strategy, income from taxes will indeed decrease in the short term, but as trade – and profits (in absolute value) – increase, so more tax income will accrue to the state, even if it is less in pure tax rate percentage terms. Therefore, it is a better bargain for everybody than the government or establishment suggestion.

The same thing happens during the brainstorming of an autocratic group,[130] where some of the better creative ideas are not aired, as the authors of the ideas do not raise them for fear of being criticized. Fortunately, since the new idea is a cognitive schema, the urge to share it guarantees that this does not often happen.

These phenomena have been understood for a long time, which is why there is protection of minority opinions. Therefore, to increase the number of available solutions and their diversity, opinions suggested by only a few people will be pre-

---

coins, can function as such a random input
[128] a so-called adverse budget
[129] the person who impersonates the group's creativity and who can step out of a certain frame of thinking, an 'out-of-the-box' thinker
[130] for example, a group with autocratic or dictatorial management

sented in the decision-making process, but will be derided. Civilized, democratic governments patronize their minorities for similar reasons, as although it is often disconcerting to care about their opinion, a longer-term view shows that their activity expands the repertory of available answers to the demands of world economics and politics.

Let us examine group decisions through an example: a group of ten people reaches a point where they can choose from three directions: left, right, and straight ahead. They have an intuition that the aim is somewhere to the right and forward, but the target in reality is to the left. Say that, at this time, six of them want to go forward, three to the right, leaving one person who wants to go to the left. According to the rules of democracy, they will vote; six win against four, and they go forward. If there is a debate, the 'forward' and the 'right' will debate, the one who voted for the left will not even have an opportunity to speak unless…

o the group has a system which protects minority opinions; or
o he stops the decision-making process,[131] and begins to market his opinion by trying to convince others that he is right.

He may attract attention by speaking louder, or being more persistent. This behavior might even be considered aggressive. Moreover, if he does this repeatedly and comes to the wrong result, they will see him as an aggressive person.

However, the real conclusion can be drawn in the opposite way: why are there not Paradisiacal conditions where nobody is aggressive and everybody agrees on everything? Why do we not just talk, vote, smile, and move on? Aggression often increases the group's creativity by turning our attention to such minority reports, which may potentially lead to the optimal decision. In many cases, emphasized, stubbornly repeated minority reports are disturbing phenomena, yet optimal decisions have to be made, notwithstanding arguments, in a calm manner.

There are two types of such aggressive manifestations:

o when somebody becomes aggressive for hormonal or other emotional reasons,[132] and surprises all of their circle. Mostly, this kind of aggression has a "meta-role" that comes from being a member of the group, and serves the goal of finding a new role within the group by showing new characteristics and features of the person.
o when a group member obtains important (acquired or constructed) information, and this situation is coupled with commitment to the group. Therefore, the person wants to share the new information at all costs, since if the group makes the idea its own and uses it, the person's Self will expand as he achieves a better position within the group and will be able to control his companions who function as his social Environment. The simplest example of this is when somebody shouts: "I have found it!" or "I have the solution!"[133]

---

[131] by any kind of unexpected behavior, for example, crying, shouting etc.
[132] a trauma behind one of his memories, or an awful association etc.
[133] "Eureka" is the classic story when Archimedes discovered the buoyancy, jumped out of the tub naked and ran around town shouting Eureka=I have found it! This called the attention of others to himself, to share the connection between the weight of the expelled fluid and the weight of the body – a radical discovery then –

Aggression: the forms in which it is manifested

Sharing pro-social and anti-social aggression

As its name implies, the basis of the division is aggression's relationship with society. In other words, the social benefit – or otherwise – of aggression. If it is useful, we talk about pro-social aggression; if it is harmful, about anti-social aggression. As soon as we relate to such complex concepts as society, several points of view are immediately raised: what is considered useful by whom,[134] and what is not. We can invariably find a group within society which at least understands, and might well support, different forms of aggression. Let us examine it through two examples of aggression, the judgment of which is obvious for the everyday reader:

o Terrorists explode a bomb. When innocent people are killed by a group of fanatics, the majority will label it as deeply anti-social aggression. In spite of this, terrorists usually represent[135] the interests of minority groups, so we can be sure that the close environment of the terrorists will make them consider it as pro-social aggression. They will see that, rather than innocent people, the dead are representatives of the enemy, and they think this justifies the issue under discussion. They see the whole act as a final possibility, a cry for help from defenseless people who have no tools to fight the numerical superiority other than the tools of intimidation

o Soldiers fight to protect, or create, democracy. Democracy is one of the basic values of Western society, so protecting it is a positive act, useful not only for the country that is becoming democratic, but also makes for a better conscience in Western societies generally. So, it is pro-social aggression. However, citizens of a non-democratic country, who lived in peace until a foreign country invaded their country, destroyed everything, killed neighbors and friends, will classify it as obviously anti-social aggression. Since they do not know of democracy and its benefits, they have no idea what the soldiers talk about; all they see is devastation.

Before reading the above examples, mention of 'terrorist' would bring a negative reaction to mind. Possibly, 'soldier' might have obtained a positive reaction. After demonstrating the relativity of these obvious concepts – according to what we consider as social norms – must we still have to reject the pro-social and anti-social division of aggression?

No, as FIPP provides a distinction that makes the division free of values. What we must keep in mind to achieve this is that, in most cases, an aggressive act is performed to achieve a goal. This goal is believed to make a positive change in the lives of one or more people; in other words, it helps their Self-expansion. For instance, the terrorist who kills in order to cause Self-expansion in members of the

---

with more and more people

[134]   or more precisely, by which group of society

[135]   or believe they represent

group he represents.[136] A soldier kills in the name of democracy to safeguard those at home, and to ensure that the next generation of citizens of the foreign country will live a less Self-narrowed life in a democratic atmosphere.

However, what of the bank-robber who walks into the bank by himself, shoots a cashier, and leaves with the money? He only cares about his Self-expansion: the moment when he spends the money – obtained at the cost of blood – and provides himself with that Self-expansion.[137] The situation would be completely different if he shared the money amongst those poor who needed it, as Robin Hood did. Then, although it is 'blood money', he would provide many more people with Self-expansion.

One way or another, the person who performs the aggressive act provides both himself and his social Environment (the people who are important to him) with Self-expansion. However, in parallel with this, Self-narrowing also appears, which he must bear as well. This Self-narrowing has two sources:

o systems established and controlled by the state,[138] which serve to preserve the power of the majority in a country; their direct aim is Self-narrowing. These include:

o acceptable punishment;

o the process of criminal investigation[139] and the accompanying anxiety[140]; and

o accusing attitudes and exclusion (nobody is happy when there is a criminal in the company or social circle)

o taking over the Self-narrowing of the victims of aggression and their Environment[141] through empathy (involuntarily). No matter whether the aggressor wants it or not, the conclusion of his acts will also be represented amongst his schemata, and these conclusions include his aggression's effect on other people. In addition, the Self-narrowing of the person who suffers the aggression will also narrow the Self of the aggressor.

On reflection, we talk about pro-social aggression when the Self-expansion we obtain with aggression is greater than the Self-narrowing arising from it. It follows that we talk about anti-social aggression when Self-narrowing is greater, and Self-expansion is smaller.

As in every concept and relationship in connection with people, we should not underestimate the role of subjectivity. Since the Self-expansions and Self-narrowings caused by the act determine the measure of Self-expansion, we have to consider several points of view.

The division of verbal and physical aggression

Previously, the police in Hungary did not intervene in family disputes unless they

---

[136]   cf. people shooting in the air and celebrating after a terrorist act
[137]   in the form of drugs, gambling, expensive sports cars, etc.
[138]   the police, or judiciary
[139]   interrogations, observation
[140]   escaping from the police, limits as to where he can go, who he can meet, which in the end narrows the Self
[141]   mourning, loss, inconvenience

were violent: the spouses could shout at each other, they could terrorize each other mentally, but the police attached aggression only to acts of physical violence (on the grounds of practicality). This example may divide physical and verbal aggression in an unhealthy way, as they are similarly represented in the brain. The power of speech can astonish us by its intensely subjective nature of human beings, and by its equality of mental processes and physical reality. Somebody swearing at another person appears to be nothing from a strictly physical point of view. But shouting in a certain tone at that other person can elicit a much greater reaction than if we, say, unintentionally collided with somebody.

Both physical events and verbal communication activate cognitive schemata in our brain, as well as our thoughts and fantasies. That is why, according to the FIPP approach, the forms of aggression are reduced to a common denominator, and why their aggression definitions show no difference. If somebody remains certain of the superiority of the physical world over mental processes, compare what would then hurt him more. What if your partner physically cheated on you once with a faceless and unknown person and she never saw that person again? Or if, although nothing actually happened, you came to know that your partner dreamed day and night in detail about how good it was to leave you for a mutual friend and start a family.

A textbook example of verbal aggression is swearing, which is nothing other than encouragement in calling for the stepping over – or on – of sexual taboos. The role of taboo,[142] from the very first, serves as an unquestionable axiom and frame of reference within the Self and society, while determining its limits. Their limiting function also means a repulsive connection towards other schemata. As an example, therefore, there is a repulsive connection between a man's schema (which represents sexuality), and the schema of his mother. Swearing is an attempt to turn it into a supporting connection with the verbal aggression's compression. Verbal aggression, with its technique of canceling compression of the limits of the Self, endangers the Self itself. For instance, if somebody is called a bastard, then his full identity is questioned. He may begin to doubt the supportive, unsullied image of his family. What may be instilled instead is rootlessness, and the fear of a vacuum in family history. In this example, the power of 'bastard' lies in the connection to the family; separation from the mother and father would endanger a central element of everybody's identity. In addition, being a bastard questions the schema of the father's persona; it questions the whole identity. In addition, identity is a concept close connected with the measure of the Self, so the faltering of identity narrows the Self, which then leads to aggression.

---

[142] untouchable, unquestionable things, acts, thoughts; stepping over them is coupled with irrational fear. for example, the taboo of incest, respecting the dead

Principal points covered in this chapter:
- aggression's negative and positive roles
- connections and what they entail
- verbal and physical violence

8. SEX

Sex says it all? * Orgasms; the long and the short of it. * Man or woman; you start.
* Women's roles. * Sex and rhythm; one method.

Sex is such a central subject of our lives and culture that it is difficult to state anything new about it. Perhaps a new viewpoint can help to discover and understand possibly unknown elements.

Several related subjects have been previously discussed, but the concept of orgasm, and intercourse itself as the central topic of sex, should be examined in detail.

Note: in this topic, the word sex is used to refer to heterosexual intercourse with vaginal penetration.

Types of orgasm

Orgasm is more or less known to psychology, but it remains an enigmatic subject. Although 1960's psychology doubted that it was true, Freud differentiated two types of female orgasm, and that they differ substantially. Clitoral orgasm can be reached by stimulating the clitoris, while vaginal orgasm is a result of vaginal stimulation.[143] Vaginal orgasm can be described as a general euphoric state, in which condition a longer lasting, so-called plateau phase, appears on the pleasure curve. In addition, vaginal orgasm elapses more slowly than does the male orgasm. Unlike male orgasm, it does not decrease sexual desire but increases libido. The resolution period[144] is much shorter as well. Compared with this, male orgasms are preceded by increasing tension; the quick dissolution of this tension is what provides men with pleasure.

Psychology talks about so many different aspects of sex that there seems to be no common denominator. However, in both the female and male, Self-expansion processes occur; these last longer in the female. Although no one person can experience the difference, male orgasms are not only shorter, but also less intense. If we examine the curve of sexual response, and the FIPP-pattern (the curve of Self-narrowing/expansion), we can identify the same stages.

---

[143]   male orgasm is said to be similar to clitoral orgasm
[144]   the "reloading" period, during which we have to rest

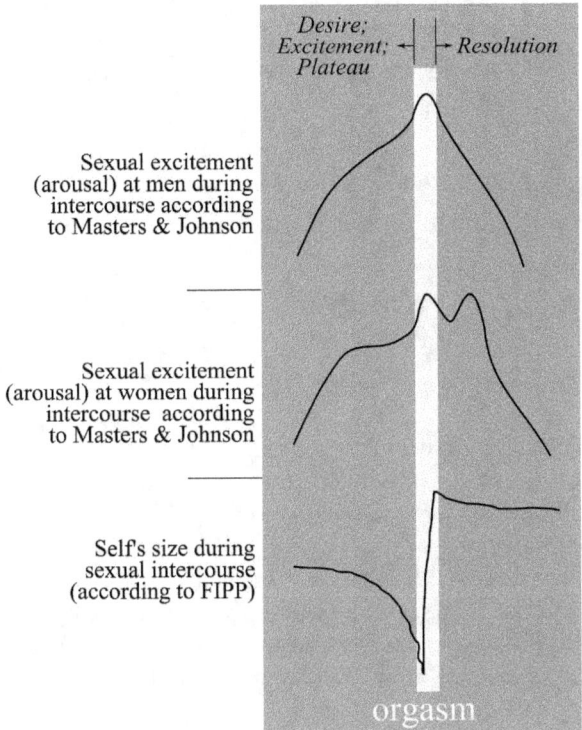

Figure 47: Curves of sexual excitement at woman and man

What conclusions can be made, apart from that they are the same process? It is plausible that the bigger the Self-narrowing, the bigger the Self-expansion. In other words: the more foreplay, the longer and greater the orgasm.

Side-effects of sex

The exaggerated emotions during and after sex[145] are connected to the social demand for Self-expansion. The blurred sense of time and space, and increased tolerance of pain, all support the existence of altered states of consciousness, which occur at the same time as the characteristics of Self-expansion are experienced.

---

[145] which are usually labeled as love, but can be desire

Excesses and absences of male and female bodies[146]

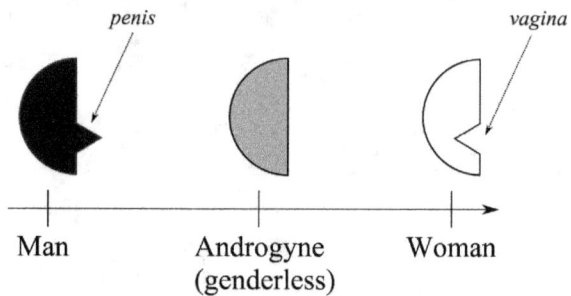

Figure 48: The male and female body viewed simply

If we try to put the physical bodies of a man and a woman on a continuum, we can imagine a genderless person[147] in between them.[148] Furthermore, that the place of man and woman will be symmetrical, compared with this sexless human.

Why is this interesting? Because in most cultures, body signs referring to sexuality are usually hidden in everyday life (ignoring explicitly man-woman interactions such as courting or seduction). So, in mentioning the human being in general, we imagine this genderless person. Similarly, when we recall our body's shape, the reference point is the sexless person's body. Compared with that, men have some excess, and women some absence, in their bodies.

This sensation is also strengthened by two further phenomena: a.) the genitalia are not part of our everyday body-image (we do not use them in everyday life as we use the other parts of our body, so we can ignore them); and b.) the genitalia react to our hormonal changes, and can be perceived as independent entities and out of control.[149]

The feeling of having something extra or missing, but also strongly part of us, results in differences in behavior between the genders. We approach the same things quite differently: men want to penetrate and to change the Environment ('putting the extra body part somewhere'), it, while women behave as if they were themselves an Environment, which needs to be penetrated by a Self ('to prevent an absence'). Environment can be made attractive, which attracts looks and stares, but at the same time it is not accidental that women pay more attention to their environment in general: the interior decoration of their apartments, the garden, their own bodies.[150]

The female equivalent of male activity is that, until fairly recently, women were

---

[146]   although we can see these days that there are significant differences on what is viewed as feminine or masculine, in this chapter to make my message more understandable I did not emphasize the small nuances, but I have used the different genders in an archetypal way, as it was viewed throughout the history.

[147]   an androgyne, but not a hermaphrodite

[148]   without genitalia, similar to angels as depicted in paintings, or people dressed in over-sized overalls

[149]   the slight difference being that, in men, this behavior is more visible

[150]   make-up, clothing etc.

seen as being unable to take the initiative, but could provoke a man into taking that initiative. A woman cannot penetrate another's Environment/Self; conversely, heterosexual men have a horror of others penetrating them. Men do not penetrate an unattractive Environment with pleasure, despite its being virtually risk-free if the person's Self-boundaries are intact (meaning that the man's personality is healthy). Women's selectivity is explained by their unwillingness to let anyone within their Self-boundaries, as that person can then merge with the Self and influences it directly. Perhaps this direct influence is why women are more affected emotionally by sex: since they let somebody into themselves, and this condition can harm them, but can also make them more valuable. Men as protagonists can let loose maximum energy through his actions, ignoring those times when he is exposed to unexpected effects as a result of the weakness of his Self-boundaries (cf. delusion, unexpectedly falling in love, decrease of self-confidence).

With this model, we can reduce the non-professional roles of women (mother, housewife), and their roles in sexual connections, to a common denominator:

o women as mothers also function as the Environment from the viewpoint of a baby's Self;[151] and

o as housewives, women secure the warmth of home as Environment for the man and the children.

To summarize, we can say that women are the passive agents of the Environment, while men can be paralleled with the Self. As we have seen, one determines the other; in other words, one does not exist without the other. A woman is needed so that the man can feel as a man, and vice versa. This is theoretically demonstrable by the division of roles in homosexual relationships. In both lesbian and male homosexual relationships there is usually a masculine, active party, and a feminine, passive party.[152]

The rhythm of the sex act

Many people have meditated on why the act of sex, intercourse, cannot be simpler, if its biological aim is solely reproduction. To ensure that sperm meets the egg efficiently, it would be enough that a penis ejaculates sperm into the vagina and onto the orifice of the uterus. The existence of the penis and the advantage of its penetration is not questioned; like a hypodermic needle needed to get a fluid to a protected place, it is evolutionary beneficial if the man can get his DNA to its target more precisely with the help of the penis.

However, the forward and backward movement of the penis in the vagina is not required to achieve this. Theoretically, it would be enough to insert the penis, inject the sperm, and take it out. However, this would make the selection of a partner, a

---

[151] the same set-up as in the sexual relationship, the difference being only that the infant takes the place of the entity needing an Environment

[152] this was not established merely to undertake the technical implementation of sexual pleasure; these roles are also manifested in sexual acts

mate, too accident-prone, and as such it would be against evolution. By this, I mean that the choice of a partner would not be well founded, and the parents' subsequent relationship would not be so stable. It would be enough for just one party to want sexual intercourse: consider how easily and quickly a male stranger can get a woman pregnant, or how easily a woman can get herself pregnant by a male; perhaps 10 seconds would be all the time that requires. Therefore, we can state that evolution, through the time-consuming nature of sex acts, and the demand for a mutual effort, reduces the number of offspring accidentally produced. In addition, it is beneficial from the standpoint of natural selection that children are created by couples who have, at least, passed this small test. If a couple are incapable of cooperating for just the few minutes the act of sex requires, then they should not have children, as they do not have the minimal criteria required of a stable couple.

If evolution imposed time limits and some sort of cooperation to creating a child, the question then arises...what is the simplest, most primitive act that demands these basic conditions.[153] In humans, the answer to this question is the effort of rhythm. This partly requires atonement,[154] and partially proves the existence of physical ability.[155] The passive act, namely a couple spending time together without any particular activity, would not of itself prove physical fitness.

I have assumed that the biological background, where hormonal processes and muscle functions regulate the connections of rhythm, ejaculation and orgasm, is already known. Nevertheless, the psychology of the process is less understood. What, then, is the answer to...why does the rhythmical movement lead to orgasm?

It is important to understand that, here, rhythmical movement is an in-out movement during which the distance between two people decreases and increases. This increasing and decreasing distance repeats the experience of the merging of Self and Environment with growing intensity. This merging of Self and Environment is best illustrated by (the initial) penetration.

From this point of view, the movement performed during intercourse is as if the partners are seeking to repeat, with growing intensity, the merging of Self and Environment made by the penetration, but without ending the merging, without separating. It is at this point where the biological and psychological functions are connected. Rhythmical repeats are there, presumably, to multiply the strength of the singular experience, just as when neurons often transmit the strength of the stimulus, by repeating the rhythmical firing with an increasing speed, as they can signal it in no other way.[156] Increasing intensity not only demonstrates the merging of Self and Environment, but also the aspiration of becoming an identical entity.

This is in tune with the aspiration – which appears in many cultures – to revert

---

[153] spending a certain amount of time together, the measurement of time required, and the ability to attune their efforts towards a mutual goal

[154] on both the physical and mental level

[155] by demonstrating the ability to make a persistent effort

[156] for example, the neurological aspect of the sense of pain

to the ancient 'Paradise' condition, when man and woman were one.[157] Another association of this aspiration, emphasized by modern psychology, is that there is a woman in every man, and vice versa.[158] That harmony and mental health comes from the unison of these parts, while suppressing none of them.

Although men and women, in connection with their orgasms and roles, are different, and they experience the sexual act differently, they both experience Self-expansion during penetration, as their Selves merge with the Environment that exists in the form of the other person. The growth of this Environment was what caused the strengthening Self-narrowing that ended after the orgasm.

Principal points covered in this chapter:
- sex, foreplay, orgasm, and their evolution
- women's roles

---

[157] for example, Eve was part of Adam's body as the rib; we can find the same aspiration in Greek mythology as well

[158] cf. Jung animus and anima

9. WHAT MAKES A RELATIONSHIP WORK?
HOW SHOULD WE CHOOSE A SPOUSE?

The symbiotic couple. * Couples and rhythm, another method. * Domination or submission; you lead. * Virtues and vices of Self-sacrifice. * Orgasmability: was that it; or was it good for you? * Picking a partner; what's the choice? * A partner as a dependant. * Man as woman and vice versa. * IQ and class differences as partnership impediments. * Can you afford a partner?

The framework communication model

FIPP can also provide interesting conclusions on the relationships of couples, as explored in the chapter on sex. Perhaps one further matter needs to be considered besides FIPP (and this is the key issue of every form of interaction between two people), namely the issue of communication.

During communication, nobody can be sure how the things he says or communicates are represented in the other person's head.[159] During communication, a schema is activated in the speaker's head. It is then translated into the speaker's spoken words, and these words activate schemata in the listener's head. There is no certainty that the two schema will be the same. To make it happen, the speaker needs to consider, at the moment of translating the schema into the spoken word, just what schemata his words may activate in the listener.

All these processes are interesting in the discussion of relationships of couples, as these automatic translation processes (from schemata to words and vice versa) build on previous experiences (discovered misunderstandings, common experiences), and become increasingly effective. They may even reach the level where couples (or spouses) who know each other well, will understand each other from a single frown, or a look, or tone; they do not need words, and yet the effectiveness of their communications is complete.

Complete, but not perfect. It is possible that communication is far above average. However, until the schemata in use are not perfectly the same, nor perfectly connected in exactly the same way, and until they use a perfect language (one which translates their schemata perfectly), it will always be that a word will activate a schema different to that which activated the word. Unfortunately, no matter how much they like and understand each other, or how much they try to avoid it, there will always be a certain distance between them that cannot be bridged. The meas-

---

[159] for example, someone comparing a woman's leg with that of a fawn, intending to woo her by pointing out their gracefulness and shapeliness, and the woman thinking that he is joking about the hairiness of her legs, and becomes upset

ure of this distance fluctuates. Sometimes it even provides the subjective experience that it seizes.[160]

This fluctuation can be connected to what Erik Erikson[161] calls hesitation between isolation and intimacy. Spouses may want to be very close to each other, but at the same time may wish to stay away from each other, to preserve their identities. If this fluctuation and distance were not there, couples could merge once and for all.[162] The relationship of spouses also has an inner life, similar to the relationship of the Self and Environment. Just as in Self-expansion and Self-narrowing, there are also situations in which couples seem to be inseparable, and sometimes where they appear to be on the edge of explosion (divorce).

Dance and rhythm – Adaptation to each other

To understand the establishment of couple relationships, let us adopt dancing as an analogy. We may know people who have no sense of rhythm. We could imagine this as...in order to catch the proper rhythm, we should do something in the next few seconds. An example would be the cha-cha: 1, 2, 2, 4, 5.[163] Compared with this, people with a faulty sense of rhythm – or none at all – would dance those steps in the wrong time: 1, 1.75, 2.5, 3.25 etc. Even worse is when the differences of time between steps are not constant: 1; 1.8; 2.1; 3.3 etc.

The rhythm of music or drums is there to guide two people into attuning their movements; for example, the drum continually emits sounds. What about people who are regularly late, or too fast, on the step (either contrary to the rhythm or independent of it)? The one who keeps to the rhythm of the music will stumble with the other person, or they step on each other's feet. Even those who – theoretically – accorded with the rhythm, will not enjoy the common activity (dance). Since we consider both parties as equal,[164] we cannot decide which one of them is not following, or cannot follow, the rhythm. But everybody sees that there is no harmony, that their movements are not synchronized and do not flow. There are two possibilities to make their movement harmonize:
- o the one with a poor sense of rhythm has to find the rhythm
- o the one with a good sense of rhythm – or who does not ruin the rhythm – speeds up or slows down to find the other's rhythm (thus both of them will then dance against the rhythm).

What conclusions can be drawn from this? Someone not following the rhythm does not mean that they dislike dancing. If the partner makes the same mistakes

---

[160] the tool for it is sex, which provides total physical fusion

[161] Erik Erikson, (1902–1994). Danish-American developmental psychologist and psychoanalyst, best known for his theory on the social development of humans, and for coining identity crisis. Briefly, Erikson postulated eight steps that a 'normal' human should encounter, confront and overcome, from infancy to late adulthood. Each step completed would build upon the earlier stages. Those steps not successfully completed...would probably reappear as problems at some time

[162] even then, their experiences after the merger would establish different schemata in each of them

[163] when it is 00:01, 00:02, 00:03 etc. on the clock

[164] for example, we see them equal when we do not hear the music but only watch them dancing

(according to the same pattern), then they both look successful at what they are doing. But to achieve this one needs a partner who:

a.) makes exactly the same mistakes; or

b.) has a higher (mistake) tolerance, so that they do not sense the time shifts so intensely.

Domination and submission

There is another point in dancing: one party dominates, the other[165] lets herself be led. If someone leads the dance exactly the way the other needs,[166] the result will be successful. A good dancer can be recognized from the wide range of movements used in attuning with the partner, of dominating and of being dominated, so that they are much more flexible in adapting to achieve mutual success.

As we can see, two things count: to be able to dominate (lead) and to accept domination. This could be described as...I give the correct commands at the right moment in time to my partner, but if they never follow them on time, that would count for nothing. So, I must give commands the same amount of time and earlier, as my partner is (usually) late in making the correct movement happen on time.

Let us return to our bad dancers. If someone has a bad sense of rhythm, will he never enjoy dancing? Far from it. He has to find the dancer who is as late or as early as he is. This is the parallel between dancing and couple relationships: nothing is perfect, yet most of us find a partner.

Fitting together

Everybody has faults. Bluntly, everybody has personality problems. Even more crudely, everybody is sick. There is no perfectly healthy person, just as there is no single truth. One reason is that different situations require different abilities. Similarly, different people require partners who, from other viewpoints, are tolerant or make different mistakes. An unskilled cook would wish that her husband's taste buds did not work properly.[167] There are people who have low sensitivity to the taste of salt (they have fewer taste buds for salt). This person requires a wife who always adds a lot of salt to their food.

Based on the above, we can say, for example, that a narcissistic person needs a self-sacrificing partner. Perhaps there is nothing interesting in this. However, although we may feel sorry for self-sacrificing people, they feel the need to surrender their personalities, so they look for narcissistic people. An extreme example of mutually satisfying needs is the sado-masochistic couple. Everyone feels sad for masochists. The absurdity of the situation is well illustrated by a joke. A masochist asks the sadist: "Hit me! Hit me!" The sadist smilingly says "Nooo! Nooo!" (He

---

[165]   in accordance with the rhythm
[166]   with the proper force and timing
[167]   or that he had none

causes pain by not satisfying the masochist's need for pain, and derives pleasure from causing that pain.)

Orgasmability

With no empirical examination, but based merely upon everyday experience and stereotypes, the submission of a new concept is allowed, a new personality trait: orgasmability. As will be seen, the concept does not completely lack a psychological basis, as I believe that it is related to hypnability. A thoroughly examined property of people, hypnability is the measure of how fast and deep one can enter hypnosis. An analogy of this is the concept of orgasmability, which describes how fast someone can achieve an orgasm, and how intense, subjectively, his or her orgasm is. According to my assumption, these two concepts (hypnability and orgasmability) are closely correlated. Both of them are connected with the ability of tuning in to the Environment. Orgasmability is linked with the widespread observation of gynecologists that women differ in how much vaginal moisture (lubrication) is produced at the same levels of excitement; men differ in how much they can suppress their sexual interest, and how high their libido is.

Turning to everyday observations, at one end of the scale there are cold, frigid people. Yet Latin nations are stereotypically viewed as more emotional and that, consequently, their citizens[168] have more passionate sexual lives; they are seen as of the other end of the scale.

Accordingly, orgasmability may be the most conspicuous property of people. The reason why it does not come to the fore is that observing it is not supported culturally: we rarely contemplate the sexual behavior of our president, a criminal judge, or the old lady next door. No matter that we have fantasies in connection with the manifestation of this parameter, apart from some exceptions (people with great sexual experience of many partners), we can verify our assumptions from a very small sample (for example, whether a person we see in the street is as active or passive in bed as we think). More often, we test our theoretical ideas on the subject upon our circle of friends, and we usually agree here. However, these friends do not fulfill psychology's present methodology, or the criteria, of sampling.

The existence of orgasmability is obvious, and unavoidable in cases where someone not only has it, but pushes it into the spotlight in a disturbing way: they are either extremely frigid, or achieve orgasms easily. In these cases, we can assume that letting other people know that they reach the extreme values of orgasmability, has a positive effect on their mental balance. Further, that he/she hopes they will profit from the existence of this property. (For example, an attorney or a nun tries to suggest reliability and steadfastness with their low orgasmability, while high orgasmability can be used to signal promiscuity or artistic talent.)

We heed this parameter, even if not necessarily consciously of it, when we are looking for a partner. There is an interval within this trait for everyone, during

---

[168] partially proved by surveys examining sexual habits

which other people can be found to be attractive. People within this interval arouse our interest instinctively, especially if they fit some of the basic parameters.[169]

However, filtering by basic parameters not only precedes, but is also connected with, orgasmability: the importance of orgasmability decreases with age, a certain stature marks the measure of this in a person.[170]

Due to its connection with sexuality, orgasmability also entails strong emotional effects: in cases of a high value, it means an affectionate or arbitrary person; in those of a low value, an aloof, distant person. This distinction connects with the desired measure of our Selves: those who fear for their Selves, if they are afraid that something will stick to or penetrate it, will look for a colder person as a partner, who approaches them less intensely. Those who see their Selves as too big, as something which grows by itself,[171] need a partner who occasionally reduces their confidence, and cuts their Selves down a little. People who are incapable of fast Self-expansion, or who need to feel that they can have a strong effect on their Environment, will need someone who expands fast, someone who can frequently achieve orgasm, reaching high levels quickly even from a low level, etc.

Economy of relationships

Choosing a partner is also a market: the product and the price is written on our faces, even if we do not see or notice it. If we take a good look at someone, we can 'see' the one sentence which describes them.[172] These sentences, despite being relatively simple, contain the demand and supply at the same time. It is not true that anyone can pick anyone else. Even preparing to be able to be chosen is an active process.[173] Although some people seem to choose actively, their limitless freedom to choose whoever they want is apparent: they cannot choose from everybody. Firstly, they collect those who let themselves be chosen, and naturally they choose from them. Musicians have legendary sexuality. It is said that a member of the Beatles could have any woman...apparently! He had the advantage, compared with an 'ordinary' man, of access to those ladies who loved his music. For example, an old lady with an orientation to classical music, and who loathes loud popular music, might expel any popular singer from her house. This belief, that there are people who can have anyone, is a typical result of an incorrect methodological conclusion: we examine a sample unrepresentative from the outset, since it was filtered by something. Then we draw a conclusion on a more general subject.

So, orgasmability is a good common denominator in finding partners, if we constantly bear in mind that everybody wants a maximum amount of orgasms for a

---

[169] for example, age, height, physical features

[170] cf. being extremely thin or anorexic has been associated with being frigid, while plump, overweight people are seen as more emotional and physically demonstrative

[171] like the teeth of rabbits and mice

[172] a sort of unconscious self-description. For example, "I want to be approached by a man who is rich and who pays attention to appearances"; or "I consider myself so beautiful that only the most perfect people should dare to talk to me"; or "I'm so lame that I need a strong man/woman next to me or I am lost", etc.

[173] when people dress up, indicating that they are attractive and ready to be chosen

certain level of self-involvement.

Orgasmability is perhaps one of the strongest keys when choosing a partner, but there are others. Some of these are:

o mental diseases, personality distortions
o a particular combination of intellectual abilities[174]
o social status.

Detour on mental illness, and its role when choosing a partner

Defining dependency

If we thoroughly examine the introduced FIPP, it turns out that such concepts as dependent personality do not exist. If we want to use it, we have to consider everybody as a dependent person. This again makes the concept of dependent personality unusable. In clinical psychology, people are termed dependent if they undertake a certain behavior to excess, and escape to it from real life. Dependency is a collective term for drug addicts, heavy smokers, alcoholics, gamblers, pathological shoppers.[175] Different theories explain what happens to control functions;[176] early mother-child connections were damaged, and so forth.

Indeed, every person is an addict: we are dependent on Self-expansion. Only our methods are different. Some people combine methods, or use different strategies to achieve Self-expanded states. For example, sometimes using sex, sometimes problem solving, at other times altruism, or charitable donations. Others do not change their ways. Perhaps we could better consider addicts as good or bad game strategists: some people always bluff, other people always 'say' the truth in poker. The winning strategy is the mixed solution: usually saying the truth but occasionally mixing in a few bluffs.

I have some concerns with the use and definition of the phrase "dependent personality". Diagnoses accord with the social attractiveness of the result of behavior, and do not focus on the cause: was not Mother Theresa an altruism addict? Is not the obsessed researcher a discovery addict? If everyone looked into themselves, they will find those techniques used to reach their everyday Self-expansions. These techniques depend on the brain. Results are provided to some people only by drugs, to others through promiscuity, or Self-sacrificing maternal care. Amongst these, some cost more, some are more visible to the outside world (more difficult to conceal), and some are considered socially useful. So, we welcome them, rather than putting them into the same category as the heavy drinker's alcohol dependency.

Let us examine an obsession which at first seems funny, but is quite sad: kleptomania.[177] We know that kleptomaniacs do not steal for the value of the objects, but

---

[174]   good memory with low intelligence; high creativity with bad visual memory etc.
[175]   who shop only for the pleasure of shopping and getting, not for a material need
[176]   which should normally stop these acts
[177]   an obsession with stealing

for the excitement of stealing and the pleasure of possession. Let us imagine an old lady affected by this disease. Preparing for stealing,[178] and the act itself,[179] is a Self-narrowing process, whereas the gaining of possession causes Self-expansion.[180] Is it possible that the lady has no other opportunity to obtain Self-expansion? Perhaps her intellectual abilities are incapable of allowing her to enjoy paintings or literary works. Sex may be out of the question. But she can still steal. Perhaps her parents, when forbidding her to steal, indoctrinated her so much with the idea of respecting property, that it causes her huge Self-expansion to violate this taboo. Once she tried it, she realized that that is what she most likes, so she enforces this strategy. We do not have to search for neurological alterations or a change in neurotransmitter systems. We need only reduce the measure of the taboo in order for her not to experience such disproportionate Self-expansion. It also shows that prohibition is not the proper remedy, as it only increases the taboo and, indirectly, the Self-expansion.

Mental illness

Let us return to choosing a partner. I indicated earlier that personality distortions and mental illnesses are of help in choosing a partner. Regardless of what we call it, it seems logical that, if someone has a weakness, he looks for a person with whom he can live his life despite having this weakness. As an extreme example: if my stomach is twice the normal size, I will then look for a person who is an excellent cook, so that he/she can cook excellent food for me. Or a person with an equally large appetite, so that we can eat together as often – and as much – as we like. I deliberately chose an extreme example: it could have been an example of extreme sexual desire and its toleration, or with being pedantic or easy-going.

Reviewing the answer to the question of the dependent personality, we can say that everybody looks for a partner with the same life strategy,[181] or whose life strategies do not cross those of the other. Further, that they help each other, in any way that leads to Self-expansion. We have to expand our perspective with one more thing: it is not only our own Self-expansion strategies that count when we plan for or dream of a life rich in Self-expansion. A relationship can be compared to (as in symbiosis) giving Self-expansion to each other, as in a barter deal: I like to listen if somebody sings and I am bored with the subject of money. You need money and it means nothing to you to sing all day, so you sing all day long.

Parts of abilities exclude others: for example, we cannot be at once both tall and short. If we were, we would be mediocre at everything. We cannot be a man and a woman at the same time. Also, different techniques of Self-expansion are available for men and women. Probably via a somewhat different route, but for the same reason, Jung reached the concepts of animus and anima.

---

[178] as it requires focusing, planning, and it is stressful
[179] it is done under time pressure, and results in high levels of adrenaline
[180] the Self became richer with the stolen object
[181] someone who seeks Self-expansion via the same methods

Animus and anima

Animus and anima are the Latin terms for the male and female spirit. According to Jung's statement, there is a man in every woman (animus) and there is a woman in every man (anima). In Jung's opinion, the condition of mental health is the harmony of two spirits in one body: so that the woman accepts that she has masculine thoughts. The man accepts that he can become overtly emotional; tears come to his eyes if he sees a child stroking a dog, or during a poignant moment in a book or film. To attain and maintain mental health, a man has to accept his anima, and a woman her animus.

We can go further than Jung. It is not difficult to notice that there are different techniques for Self-expansion according to different genders – manifested in the animus and the anima – and the cognitive schema which can be accessed and activated by them. In the case of anima it might be music, a child, etc.; in animus, strength, competition; and so forth. In order to be able to produce new Self-expansions, we cannot limit ourselves to our gender's half of the opportunities. Regardless of how good our techniques are: a.) we may use up all our possibilities after awhile, and the technique begins to cause increasingly smaller Self-expansions;[182] b.) we become completely one-sided, and use our techniques to affect every part of our lives;[183] or, c.) when the frames are so expanded that it threatens us with annihilation.[184]

Intellectual ability

As a head hunter, I have interviewed many people for different jobs throughout my career. Flexibility was the declared expectation of many clients, together with creativity. As a classical psychologist, I would have been supposed to take some creativity tests and test – and tire – applicants with them. Questions arise: what exactly do creativity tests measure; and what type of creativity was it that my clients required. Instead, I decided to examine their ability to change viewpoints. Perhaps I might have found a test for this, so what remained was to confront them with spontaneity. During the interview, I frequently changed the subject, sometimes to one completely unconnected with the subject of the job. Then, not impolitely, I might get up from the table and do something unusual: walk out of the room, tell jokes, open and shut the window etc. In the meantime, I was curious as to how quickly they adapted to the new situation, and how much what I did confused them. On many occasions the speed, topics and vocabulary of the conversation showed me that there is no possibility of using these tricks. At other times, a funny or jokey association was enough to show that there was no appropriate response to it (a typical 'free shot' situation); I was the measuring instrument. If they

---

[182] for example, someone likes climbing mountains, but cannot afford to travel any farther than the little hill of his village which he can scale blindfolded; that is then a problem

[183] for example, when someone risks his job or marriage or existence to climb mountains

[184] for example, when we begin to climb Everest with a bad vascular system, simply because we have climbed everything else

could follow, or maybe even surprise, me, then I could be sure my clients would then consider the applicants intelligence, flexibility, etc.

A friend spontaneously gave selected women weird presents at university parties; he made flowers out of napkins, or something out of a match. Those who appreciated creativity were worth doing something for him. How does this fit in with long-term relationships (professional or private)? The main point of attuning to each other is to show whether the partners can relax in each other's company, or how they respond to each other's creativity. They can spread the new cognitive schemata established in their Self-expansions. Moreover, they can build new cognitive schemata on each other's schemata, which causes Self-expansion for both of them. These new cognitive schemata can be painful puns, dry humor, beautiful rhymes, poetic images, mathematical formulae, new ballet steps, or musical tunes. The point is to be able to provide the other with Self-expansion, by producing cognitive schemata during their communication. That newly-created cognitive schema has to be new and usable for the partner. It does not matter whether this happens at the workplace during a brainstorming session, or in a dance hall, or between jazz musicians who have spontaneously gathered to improvise.

This is another way of choosing a partner in life.

The other extreme of choosing a partner is when we at least do not have to be afraid that the partner causes, or will cause, Self-narrowing. A person who holds himself in high esteem, but who has weaker abilities, will be anxious if he is unable to follow his partner whom he also holds in high esteem; say in music, sport or conversation. If I meet Michael Jordan to play 2-on-2 street ball, his being much better than me will not be my only problem. It would make me nervous that perhaps I should not be his partner, as I do not know even the most basic techniques. If I make myself believe that I am an excellent physicist and able to talk to Einstein or Hawking, then I will feel small and embarrassed, as I would not be able to understand him (I Self-narrow), and he has to make increasingly lower-level schemata in order not to end the conversation. This will be inconvenient for him, as he does not obtain any Self-expansion. However, if I stand with a person who is more or less on the same level as myself, perhaps what we talk about will not be so inspiring, but at least I do not narrow myself. And I will try to expand my Self in other fields of life.

The concept of creativity is too complex and multidimensional to be of use.[185] Sometimes, classic creativity is not what the establishment of a new schema requires: to recall a part of a poem suitable for a situation requires long-term memory, a strategic game requires thorough planning, music requires good musicality, dancing requires a good sense of rhythm and co-ordination of movement, etc. That is why creativity and intelligence are not the only things that count in choosing a partner or employee. Rather, it is the compilation of these abilities. Of probably equal importance are personality and communication. A good result can be broadcast with insulting arrogance (bigheadedness), and a major mistake can be

---

[185]   there is visual and acoustic, originality, out-of-the-box-thinking, restructuring

fixed with charm and politeness.

These viewpoints are useful in understanding the whole picture.

Socio-economic status

There is nothing particularly new in describing the role of social status in choosing partners. If a young lady wants to go home from the disco in an expensive car, these days she examines the men, what car they arrived in etc.

But money and wealth are dynamic: having a 50,000 USD car does not mean I do not have a 75,000 USD loan. An empty wallet does not mean that I have no money in the bank, or a monthly salary of 10,000 USD. As an initial approach, I believe that money in a wallet, and wealth, can be seen at a certain moment as so plastic that this source of information can satisfy only a short-term thinker.

Economic status is a superior source of information, although for those who believe in the power of money, choosing a partner based on wealth reverts to choosing a partner based on mental illness. Why? Because wealth, in most cases, is important when it is needed for a dependency.[186] The other variation is when a wealthy man or woman avoids Self-narrowing by choosing a similarly wealthy partner: so he/she will not be afraid that the merging of their fortunes will make his/her half of their combined wealth considerably smaller than what he/she is used to. This can be uncomfortable in cases of divorce, or living up to and beyond those reserves of wealth.

We should confront the question: why would economic status be important in choosing a partner? It is simultaneously important and unimportant. Economic[187] status is important, as it accompanies cultural fitting. Also, cultural background tells us something of intellectual ability, and the similarity of cognitive schemata. If I was raised in a family comparable to that of a potential partner, we will have the same experiences, and I can then provide that partner with Self-expansion when I have reactions similar to hers.

At the same time, it is not important, as most high-level Self-expansion is not dependent upon money. There again, wealth shows its importance in that a lack of money can cause much Self-narrowing.[188]

Principal points covered in this chapter:
- couples: natural selection and other selection criteria
- how – and what – two people give to each other;
- and what they take, as well as maintaining their individuality

---

[186] dependent shopping or gambling
[187] to be more exact, socio-economic
[188] frustration, conflict etc.

10. FUNCTION PRACTICE (CIRCULAR REACTIONS) AND THE DESCRIPTION OF COGNITIVE SCHEMATA

> Circular reactions = function practice = repetition, repetition. * 'Reality' as a mental representation; unsplitting the atoms. * The hierarchy of schemata; categories and their boundaries. * The schemata super-highway. * Limitations, simplifications and life 'models'. * Spur-of-the-moment Self-expansion and sharing. * Cultivating cognitive schemata and the lessons we learn. * Function practice is child's play.

What is function practice (circular reactions)?

If anyone has seen a child dirtying, then cleaning, a toy fifty times, then dirtying it again, they will know what function practice[189] is. The same practice occurs when a child learns to stand up, then falls down, then stands up again, as long as they are able to physically do so or learn how to stay on their feet. I would not limit use of the concept of function practice solely to children: when a 16-18 year old juvenile finally obtains his driving license, all he wants is to drive, and every opportunity to get behind a steering wheel will be taken.

If anyone suspects from the foregoing that the phrase "function practice" is the same as practice, they would be close to the truth. This term was invented to distinguish the everyday use of the word "practice" with a more general meaning, one based upon the phenomenon that people can be happy with things that, theoretically, are not beneficial in the short term. Moreover, that a seemingly boring thing can be endlessly repeated while enduring a deal of inconvenience, such as a child continually falling down.

To understand this phenomenon more precisely, we must examine what mental processes occur during function practice. Mental processes connect with cognitive schemata, therefore we should initially consider the nature, formation and function of these schemata.

FIPP's interpretation of the concept of cognitive schema

A cognitive schema is the key to cognitive science.[190] There is a great deal of lit-

---

[189] Jean Piaget (1896-1980), the very first psychologist who described in detail the phases of children's mental development, used the term 'Circular reactions' as a synonym for function practice

[190] science on the boundaries of biology, philosophy, neurology, psychology and informatics

erature on this subject; here is one understanding of this concept.

Previously, in other topics and, briefly, in the introduction to FIPP, a cognitive schema was described as the basic element of thinking, that it is nothing more than a mental model of a certain aspect of the outside world. So, almost everything that assists thinking can be considered as a cognitive schema: concepts, categories, theories, symbols etc.[191]

To understand the concept of a mental model, let us recall the definition of the term 'model': a model is a copy, which always copies the original thing in a simplified way. It seizes only one or two aspects of reality, and disregards other aspects or dimensions. It does all this to provide the brain, through simplification, with a manageable amount of information. The less important, but still essential, information, can predict accurately enough how the modeled entity will behave. So, we could define the reasoning of all models, and therefore the ultimate goal of cognitive schemata, as: to help with, and provide, adaptation, so that the chances of a person surviving in the outside world increase by properly representing that world. This happens in the case of every lesson learned, even on a somewhat primitive level at S-R[192] reactions. The lack of the S-R reaction, or learning, would lead to that individual's death.

If the mouse we place in a labyrinth did not model the labyrinth in his brain – for example, from stubbornness or stupidity, he did not examine what routes and crossovers there were – and so did not learn where the food was, it would eventually starve to death.

Levels of reality (and of modeling): the multiple aspects of reality

In order to understand the function of cognitive schemata, let us first take a slight detour via the relationship between reality and its mental representation.

When talking about reality, in most cases we think of a mechanical image of the world consisting of physically extant atoms, one which obeys the laws of physics. The important thing is not whether the world is like that, or whether it includes extra parts that cannot be described with atoms, but that our brain is capable of forming an image, of only limited complexity, of this mass of atoms. Our brains do not operate on the level of atoms, nor with the representation of atoms, but with relationships.

Figure 49: In reality, our world is a set of different atoms

---

[191] we could go further and imagine schemata in connection with movement and feelings, but these are disregarded here
[192] S-R=stimulus-response: the most primitive reflex-like form of learning

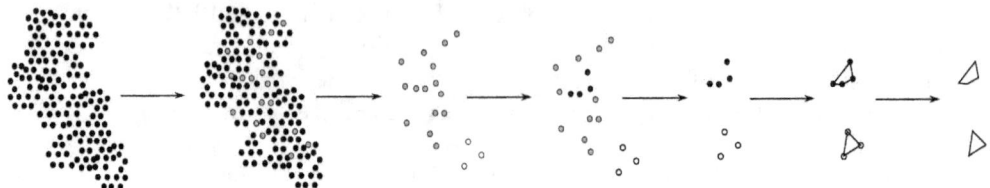

Figure 50: Reducing the amount of information

These relationships can be between atoms, but to adapt to our complete reality we must cope with the different levels of their establishment and combinations of atoms. As an example: a person may be affected by 10^{1000} atoms.[193] Of these, he might perceive 10^{100} atoms, equal to 10^{50} shapes that are combined in 1030 objects, down to one piece of the world in which he lives. Cognitive processes – even if not on an atomic level – will deal with things within the spectrum of the level of (10^{50} different) shapes to the level of one piece of universe. This presumes that it has to somehow structure these stimuli (the information), and thus the 10^{1000} atoms. Here, structuring means extracting the pattern or essence of different groups of atoms by using our mind's ability to model. As in each person these atoms group themselves differently, it is clear that our models will also differ, even if, seemingly, we talk about the same things. The difference of our models is reflected in our differing reactions to the same inputs.

Key to understanding the reason for modeling is that the functioning of our mental abilities is based upon limited mental capacity. We can readily admit that the full complexity of the universe (compared with the number of combinations of the 10^{1000} atoms) is impossible for our minds to grasp. Perhaps it is also conceivable (and parallels our everyday experience), that we can manipulate simultaneously just a few cognitive schemata. We can listen to, or concentrate fully on, just one source, while keeping several other, different, matters in our heads.[194]. Disregarding, for example, 99.5% of the 10^{1000} atoms building our outside world, and purposely not wanting to become known to those, does not seem to be an efficient strategy, as it is possible that we may be endangered by something from that 99.5% territory which we pay no attention to, or avoid. In summary, we can say that we have to live in a world where our life depends on 10^{1000} different things and our brain's capacity is able to parallel process 10^1 different things. How can we achieve this?

The answer lies in hierarchies. Hierarchies make it possible not only to sum or multiply numbers, but also to raise them to a higher power. Let us assume that we could raise our capacity by 10% at the cost of a lot of pain, beginning with, say, 10 units. But what is 10, 11 or even 20, compared with 10^{1000}? What would happen if

---

[193]   the number and order of magnitude are illustrative
[194]   as an example of the limited capacities of our mind, there is a widespread observation in psychology that our short-term memory can store only five to nine things

we could somehow double or triple our capacity? It is still 20 or 30, almost nothing compared with 10^{1000}. However, if we increase the base capacity exponentially, then we can reach $((10^{10})^{10})^{10} = 10^{1000}$ in just a few steps.

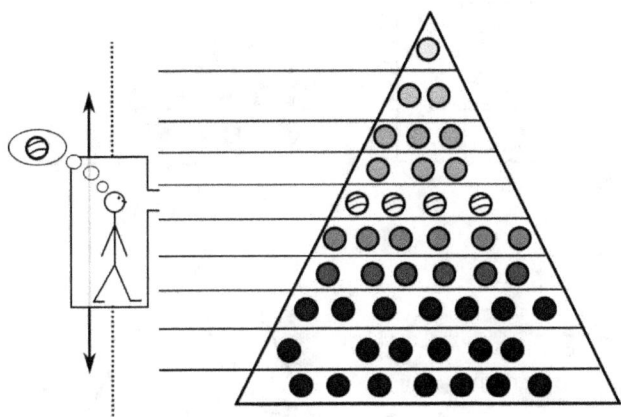

Figure 51: Ability to see different detail levels

What is modeling based on hierarchy? That the brain extracts the essence: the similarity of elements of a set with different complexity. It does the same on the levels of perception, when creating categories or establishing regularities, and when it forms paradigms. Only the units differ: at the levels of perception the unit is the physical stimuli; in categories it is the properties; in rules it is the experiences; and so on. When the similarities are extracted, these become a new element of a more complex set: firstly, the basic stimuli, then the essence derived from those, followed by the essence of those essences...to, eventually, the so-called cognitive schemata, which models a certain detail of our world.

This ability is insufficient by itself, as the constant extraction of essence results in decreasing data-like knowledge of the world; we would see fewer details with which to understand the connections. But to adapt ourselves to our environment, we need access to all information. So as not to lose the full picture, our brain needs to be able to jump, switch between, and connect matters between, levels.[195] This occurs because a particular detail may be of interest, next time the overview is important, and so forth. Moreover, sometimes one needs to view the same cognitive schema with its child-schemata. Besides this ability to move and connect between levels, two additional abilities are required to make this method function: induction and deduction.

---

[195] like an elevator (lift), connecting one at a very high level with a basic (lower) one

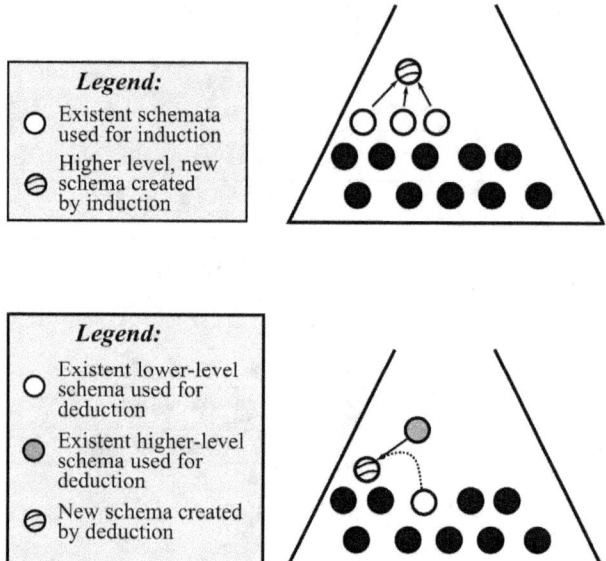

Figure 52: Induction and deduction

Induction happens when the brain extracts the essence from lower-level schemata. Deduction is when a higher-level schema, accompanied by a lower-level schema that is on the same level as the constituents of the higher one, form a new schema.

Before we accept that there is order in our brains, I should express doubt that we can talk here about a multi-story construct similar to a pyramid, where every cognitive schema understands which level it is on. I have no proof, only an intuition, that there are also schemata halfway, or one-third of the distance, between stories.

It is possible that the connections are far more chaotic than in a regular pyramid. Rather, we should imagine the world of schemata as a collection of small and large pyramids embedded in each other. However, regular pyramids will be used to illustrate the following; they provide a satisfactory model for a base.

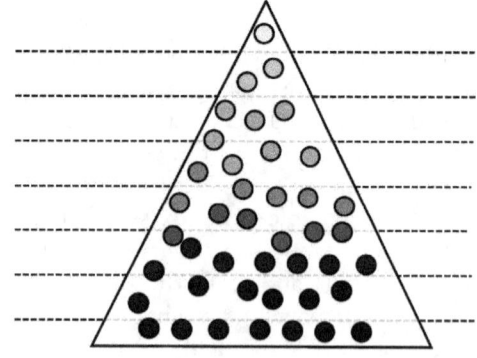

Figure 53: The leveling of the schemata is not uniform

Before examining cognitive schemata in detail, we should look at the philosophical results of connections between reality and our minds. That we cannot obtain first-hand information on the physical world, due to the boundaries of our perception,[196] is not new. Thus, by considering the above, we can state something of the reality that a person perceives. Unfortunately, nobody can prove that reality is not that you are the only person who exists in the world, and that everything you perceive is only a dream. Or that reading this is only a dream.[197] If we disregard this possibility, and presume that there are people and other entities around us, then we can also state that the outside world connects with the Self which processes its environment only in the form of those mental representations that process the information. Similarly, our effect on reality can be considered real only in that we give a command to perform an act, then nothing happens, then new information reaches us of the change – presumably as a result of that act – in our representation of the world.[198] Whether anything changed in reality, or what this change might concern, is an insoluble riddle.

In my opinion, the concept of the 'outside world' is an unfortunate construct: it is so difficult to define objective reality that it seems a pointless exercise. If we accept that reality is not necessarily the way we perceive it, then we immediately start looking on our world from the viewpoint of a being independent from everybody.[199] It is probable that these independent beings have different organs of sense, different logic, that they model the world in different ways, and may not even think on a neurological basis. However, even if we could contact them – while trying to reduce both their communicational code system and ours to a common denominator – we would inevitably build on our own logic and mental representations to understand what they see. To summarize: we have to accept that the outside world only reaches us through our mental representations. Its cognition is basically determined by our cognitive schemata, which we cannot get rid of, even if we wanted to. Perhaps we achieve the least distorted image of the outside world by recalling childhood experiences, when the majority of our cognitive schemata did not limit the way we saw, heard, felt, etc.

Cognitive schemata and ideas. Categories and their typical examples. The borders of cognitive schemata

On representing the world and categories, perhaps one should recall Plato on ideas. There are many differences and similarities between cognitive schemata and ideas. While a cognitive schema is a mental construction, the concept of ideas re-

---

196   for example, we cannot see UV light or atomic particles
197   the expanded version of this possibility is explored in the film "The Matrix", which is based upon William Gibson's books "Burning Chrome" and "Neuromancer"
198   to clarify: there is no proof that anything changes in reality as a result of our intention to perform an act. We simply perceive that we have to change our mental representations in order to comply with inputs from the world beyond our mind
199   for example, UFOs, God, gods, other transcendent beings etc.

fers to the essence of certain things. They are free from mistakes[200] and all earthly attributes.[201]

The two concepts are not the same. However, the reason this requires consideration is that we can consider an idea as the title of a cognitive schema or its theoretical designation. Plato[202] seems to have felt the essence of cognitive schemata when he wrote of generally valid things. He imagined the ideas as something perfect, and the physical objects as poor quality copies of the ideas. In our approach, cognitive schemata are more akin to a list of relations, or a set of rules: an entity which integrates the common property of every object (those that are parts of the category) under discussion. This entity is perfect in that it is a mere mental construction, and reality does not distort it with its own mistakes.

Yet cognitive schema should not be confused with the typical example of a category, which marks that element which best fits the definition of the category.[203]

These parameters/rules/definitions form the essence of each cognitive schema. As definitions of categories they are empty statements, worthless constructs, but when filled with content, new, individual elements emerge.[204] Beside these definitions, another important characteristic of cognitive schemata is their connections with other cognitive schemata. These connections can point upwards (cf. induction), downwards (cf. deduction), or can be on the same level (cf. association). We have not so far examined this last variant.

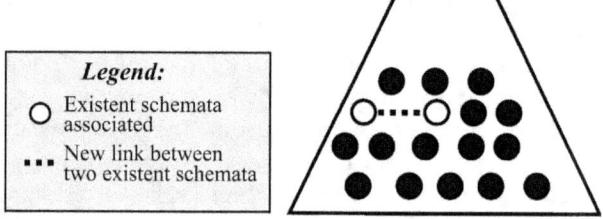

Figure 54: Association of schemata

---

[200]   the perfect circle, the perfect ball, etc.
[201]   specifics due to physical appearance
[202]   who invented the concept of ideas
[203]   the "typical example" is a psychology term depicting that element of the set forming the category which is the default example for most people, as it has some parameters closely matching the criteria of the category. According to this definition, the "typical example" of the category "pet" is the dog or the cat, and not the parrot or the turtle, as fewer people have experience of the latter animals. This does not make the typical example a perfect fit in the category, as the definition of a category is inevitably simplified. From this point, only matters which fit the parameters of the definition of the category will be members of the category. While an idea is based upon a convention, as a result of verbal thinking every word has to have the same definition for all people. Nevertheless, one example typifies how this can be interpreted by different people. For example, if I say 'ball' to a basketball player, in his head the image of the latest NBA official basketball may appear. If I say ball to a soccer player, he or she may think of the official ball for the latest World Cup
[204]   cf. with deduction

Association is that type of connection when cognitive schemata of the same rank connect with each other; the aim of that connection is simply to become a part of a model within a larger system.

Another type of connection is at least as important. Namely, those negative connections that guarantee differences. These are the connections that designate the borders of the cognitive schema. They do so by designating a group of cognitive schemata with which it has no common properties; if two cognitive schemata had common properties, they would then be connected positively by these properties. We can also see this principle in real life: we often define something by saying which things are not characteristic of it. This is important in cases when a part of the definition is not the fulfillment of a requirement, but the lack of it.[205] How these cognitive schemata can be imagined is now considered in detail.

The road network metaphor

Cognitive schemata are nothing other than connections similar to that of a road network. There are cities (which are akin to cognitive schemata) having districts within in them; this is similar to cognitive schemata forming new units by building them onto each other. There are then the main roads connecting these districts, with one, two, or three lanes, which show the strength of the connection between the cognitive schemata. The larger categories of cognitive schemata are connected like cities and towns in a country.

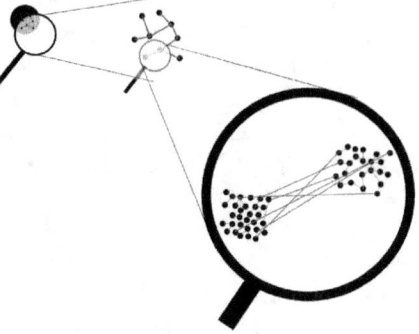

Figure 55: Within schemata we also find schemata

The analogy has two important parts:

o the connections between cognitive schemata form a hierarchical network. This means that something is not connected to something else, where the 'something' can also be a sub-network. This network and its sub-networks are similar to physics, where particles were divided into smaller and smaller parts, until finally it was realized that there was nothing else, only waves. The difference between particles and cognitive schemata is that, in the latter, we find neurons instead of waves; and

o the other is leveling: as there is also the street-district-city-country-region-continent series, here we can identify levels as well.

---

[205] for example, when we define animals as living entities that – save for the kangaroo and wallaby – walk on more than two feet; whereas people and birds have two legs, animals and insects walk on four, six, eight or more legs

Archetypes

As previously examined, the way matters are organized in the world has little or nothing to do with the way we organize the world in our heads, due in part to:

o the limits of the organs of sense;

o the simplification made by the organs of sense in translating the outside world;[206] and

o the limits of our brain capacity and its pre-wired nature and structure.

These influence how the world is represented.

The abovementioned limits seem to hinder us in adaptation, as we are not taking our decisions using all available information. This might be true, or these limitations also exist in other human beings, and aid communication between people. That others do not see in the infrared range either, or that others also do not have much greater mental capacity (and so on), enables almost identical models of the world to be made, and so we can share them.

Apart from these limits, people go through the same life phases due to their physical-biological nature: a child is born, has a mother and father, can be either male or female, experiences gravity, acceleration, collision etc. All of these limitations and common points determine the models we build.

Examples of models that are probably attached to the human species, and as such span differences in culture, include:

growing: the brain has to determine the principal direction or orientation; by following lines of gravity, up and down are perceived. Experience shows that something that is small can also become bigger, by growing. The end-products of growing range between the dwarf and the giant, as definitions of the two extremities. Following this logic, it is no wonder that the concepts of up and down, big and small, dwarf and giants etc. can be found in every culture.

God: regardless of what people think or believe about the origin of the system they find in the world,[207] the presence of a system is perceived in one way or another. The operator, the top of the system, is a cardinal point for everyone that has to be named. No matter what we call it – the Creator, a higher intelligence etc. – we are talking more or less about the same thing.

Extra-terrestrial: if we look at our environment as a system that we live in,[208] there has to be something beyond this system. In this extra-system there might be living creatures. Whether these living creatures are as an African native is to Westerners, or how a UFO is viewed by a modern man, or witches were viewed in the Middle Ages, is all the same: we exist in our system, and there is something beyond it. Also, that that something has always been named by ourselves with different names, even if nobody had seen them.

---

[206] for example, if we look at a forest, we do not see single trees

[207] our brain gives the system to the outside world; or there is a system in the outside world because a higher power built it as a system

[208] we can take the planet Earth, or a village in a jungle, as our system

Moreover, we feel fundamentally that these models are not comparable with transient modern constructs, such as, say, acid rock, or the wearing of ripped jeans, but that they carry a certain universality. For Jung, these models had a unique importance, as archaic concepts building bridges to the deepest layers of our psyche. The subconscious[209] operates using mainly these models, so they form the language of the subconscious. Jung calls them archetypes.

Spontaneous Self-expansion

A better understanding of the concept of cognitive schemata makes it possible to be understood more precisely and to explain certain exceptions. The FIPP emphasizes the process – of Self-narrowing → establishing a new schema → Self-expansion – while ignoring spontaneous Self-expansion. That is, where two schema accidentally merge through a connection and establish something new. The following example is rather tabloid-like, but it sheds light on the process of easy Self-expansion. Let us assume that somebody's favorite actress is Angelina Jolie, and their favorite actor is Brad Pitt. He respects both persons and holds them in high esteem, for their beauty and talent. Then he reads that they have married each other. Any happiness he feels about this comes from establishing the cognitive schema of a perfect couple, on the basis of the cognitive schemata of perfect stars. Of course, there is a testing phase here as well, just as we have seen in the chapter on Problem Solving. The person attempts to match the existing information on the actor and actress to determine whether their personalities fit each other and if they would form a good couple. Perhaps, if Brad Pitt had married Pamela Anderson, that would have established a more contradictory cognitive schema. From this, we can see that it took no serious effort to establish the new schema. Moreover, the fan's skills and abilities were not questioned while reading the news, so the Environment did not endanger his Self that much. Accordingly, the Self-expansion is not so frenetic either, but is enough to produce the usual sharing imperative, so he might relate this news to other friends and fans in his environment.

The establishment and growth of cognitive schemata

The essence and precondition of a cognitive schema are its inner rules. These principally define the cognitive schema, whatever it might be: a mathematical formula, a tune, or an object. Connecting this rule with other cognitive schemata, the schema becomes increasingly embedded in the net of pre-existing schemata. In other words, the cognitive schema's net of connection spreads.

From this description, it follows that there are cognitive schemata with either smaller or greater nets of connections. Those with a smaller net are therefore less determining, and those with greater networks blend with the mass of cognitive

---

[209] which plays an important role in the aetiology of psychic diseases in psychoanalysis

schemata. An example of a larger cognitive schemata is the schema of a man, or a woman, which is also connected (either positively or negatively related) with the schemata and other properties[210] of all the people we know.

The net of connections of cognitive schemata is capable not only of spreading, but also of restructuring and shrinking. They rarely vanish without trace, since they remain in the form of actual facts. Only their system of connections restructure radically, to the extent that its shape bears no resemblance to the original.

The establishment of a new cognitive schema does not expand the Self solely due to the establishment of the new connections. It is also based on the former experiences that anticipate the number of new connections to be established. For example, when an art dealer buys a Picasso for 1 million USD, he is neither happy nor unhappy. He has spent a considerable amount of money. But he is almost sure that that expenditure will enable him to sell on the painting and so make a substantial profit for himself; perhaps, at the moment of purchase, he anticipates how he will spend that profit.

Alternatively, when a new cognitive schema is established, the Self also expands as it expects a number of new connections to be created soon, which pleases it. Perhaps someone discovers a new restaurant in his neighborhood; he is happy that there is a new menu available to try. The cognitive schema of the restaurant will make new cognitive schemata of meals, which connect with the cognitive schemata of taste.

The pleasure of having established new cognitive schema accompanies the testing process previously mentioned, which examines the congruence of the world and the cognitive schema. For example, the restaurant may seem nice, but is it clean? It may be nice and clean, but are the waiters polite, civil? In order to avoid this scrutiny, and so reduce the pleasure of the establishment of the new cognitive schema, in most cases a person will:

o complete any missing information with positive things: the restaurant is nice and clean, so the toilets must also be clean. We do not eradicate our pleasure by inspecting all of the rooms to check their condition;

o examine the topic at a higher level – by making a so-called "general impression" – before going into the detail step-by-step. For example, if I often frequent Starbucks, I enter one of its outlets anticipating an understanding of its condition that I may never bother to verify. The same applies to the restaurants of a particular district of a city, or in the case of a national cuisine. If I go to a Chinese restaurant, I am more or less aware of what tastes I can expect there.

The results of testing increasingly fill and enrich the cognitive schema, resulting in a detailed picture being formed. Naturally, the enrichment of the cognitive schema cannot be reached only with the help of outside stimuli, but it also requires inner processes: we say that we are "ruminating" on a problem. At such times there is no new input, it is only the variables of the structure trying to con-

---

[210] for example, aggression, tenderness, risk taking, compassion etc.

nect with other, pre-existing and different, cognitive schemata. This happens when someone reads a theory and tries to understand it by bringing up examples, attempting to rebuild it, and so on.

Experiencing a cognitive schema that has a stable, unambiguous inner structure, and that it is connected with other cognitive schemata, provides further pleasure. Although the new cognitive schema was established earlier, henceforth it is both usable and ready to make new connections.

Once a cognitive schema is ready for use, it becomes subject to more or less intense verification when in use. Verification is either direct,[211] or meta-reflective,[212] about the value of its use.

Definition of function practice (circular reactions) with the help of cognitive schemata

This preliminary examination of understanding cognitive schemata enables us to attempt to explain the phenomenon of function practice, or circular reactions. Principally, it relates to the establishment of cognitive schemata, and the growth of their net(s) of connections. Moreover, we can also say that function practice is no more than all of those attempts to increase the net of connections that are motivated by the reinforcing effect of Self-expansion. The latter is the function pleasure that we can observe in function practice, and which has been previously described in psychology. Function pleasure is the happiness we feel when becoming increasingly successful at an ability we have to learn, or a series of acts as we use them.

However, what is the phenomenon in connection with which we can declare that we are becoming more successful?

As previously seen, after the main connections – the essence of the cognitive schema – congregate, the cognitive schema then begins to shape the system of connections that determine its relationship with other cognitive schemata. In an admittedly artificial manner, we can divide these relationships into:

o inner connections, which organize the constituents of the cognitive schema; and
o outer connections, which organize the relationships of the cognitive schema.

This division is not the best way to view the schemata, as these connections do not have to differ in quality merely for occurring within cognitive schemata. Within the cognitive schemata, there are also other cognitive schemata; recall that a cognitive schema is established through the integration of other, lower-level, cognitive schemata, or by the extraction of their essence through induction. Perhaps a method of distinguishing inner and outer connections is by measuring the strength or density of those connections. This would be similar to the road network meta-

---

[211] for example, can we solve something with it?
[212] can we solve something quicker than usual?

phor, showing roads within a city and those leading to other cities. Both inner and outer roads are similar, but while those within the city have just one or two lanes, the roads – or highways – between cities can have three or four lanes.

The greater strength of a connection is due to the inner connections of the cognitive schema having become more harmonic, so making the inner contradictions vanish. The solving of these minor, internal contradictions leads to small Self-expansions. For example, we can hit a ball with a tennis racket, but a good coach can instruct us how we can hit it with more confidence, and with greater accuracy and power. To avoid selecting incorrect methods of achieving these aims we must practice, which makes the connections stronger.

The road network metaphor can be used to illustrate two further points. That the city is already there (the cognitive schema is established) means that its road system becomes increasingly complex – the inner net of connections of the cognitive schema grows – and also has some traffic. What else can then be done to improve what we have, in order to be able to travel from one part of the city to another more quickly; how can we increase the efficiency of the modeling? To achieve this, we must do away with dead-ends, replace two-way streets with one-way streets (so dissolving mini-contradictions), and by broadening main roads (so strengthening the connections by practice). That is how it looks at the micro level of cognitive schemata.

On the behavioral, macro, level, the previously mentioned function pleasure can be observed: the better we do something, the more we initially like it, but we then become bored with it. The order of this progression is:

o initially, the child or adult cannot solve a problem

o using the trial-and-error method, he proposes a solution

o the solution is often wrong, but the proportion of good solutions begins to increase

o the proportion of good solutions almost completely outnumbers the errors, so the problem can be solved with almost complete certainty

o in dealing with the problem, boredom sets in, and:

o he stops the activity and does not begin again[213]

o it becomes a necessary, automatic, routine, undertaken by pure reflex[214]

o the problem is made more complex, testing his success at solving the more complex puzzle[215]

But rather than becoming bored, why do we stop before reaching peak (100%) performance? Why do we not strive to become completely perfect? The answer: after awhile, our investment is so much greater than the profit or advantage earned, that it seems to have become an enterprise which would provide a deficit if further investment were made in its development. Even if not a deficit, a better invest-

---

[213] in the case of a child, shaking a toy; people who retire and who do not miss their previous job, as they have reached their goal

[214] tying a shoelace, multiplying figures

[215] cycling, cycling without hands, on one wheel; operations in different numerical systems, natural numbers, complex numbers, binary numbers etc.

ment can be made in an enterprise where equal effort promises greater reward. Here, profit and effort should not be thought of as abstract numbers, rather in terms of language of the psyche i.e. Self-expansion and Self-narrowing.

Why is it like that? Repairing small mistakes in an almost complete cognitive schema requires restructuring of the whole schema. However, the increase of performance and competence, which would lead to Self-expansion, is hardly noticeable.

People who become bored with their profession do not realize that they can reach and obtain in other fields of life the Self-expansion they are used to. However, due to a failure-averse attitude, or the lack of a risk-taking attitude, they do not dare to change. They stay in the field where they are acknowledged, they do everything routinely, yet the meaning of their life, and their happiness (series of Self-expansions), is missing.

My comments on function practice could be taken as a mere by-product of human thinking. However, function practice is much more than that: it is the key to understanding thinking and human development. If someone did not want to practice functions, he would not only give up function pleasure, but would stand wholly incompetent in the world. As the establishment, growth and use of cognitive schemata are not to be separated, they take place in a continuum, and the same processes occur. Connections are established the same way, the only question being "Just where do we stand on the scale? Just above the base when the connections are established, or significantly higher following function practice?" So, although function practice was previously a good concept, closer examination shows that it is no more than the normal activity and spreading of a schemata. Being a concept difficult to define, its use should be limited to the one phenomenon, or perhaps two, necessary in child psychology.

A final detour: play as autotelic function practice

Playing is another favorite philosophical question. It has no economic profit, yet it consumes considerable energy and is seemingly undertaken with, and followed by, great pleasure. Questions arise: why is play established? How can we define it precisely? To what can we oppose it?[216] Etologists have defined play as practicing crucial behaviors[217] without any negative repercussions. Psychology describes play as a form of function practice with no specific aim.

Upon this, a key issue remains unanswered: what motivates the play; where does the most important constituent of play – pleasure – come from?

FIPP provides an answer: a great amount of information congregates in a child's head, which is stored in the form of separate cognitive schemata, the connections between which have yet to be established.[218] So, during play, an array of new cog-

---

[216] for example, doing nothing, being bored, working
[217] such as hunting
[218] example: he knows he has grandparents. He has heard about marriage. He knows that his parents are married.

nitive schemata are continually being established, which cause frequent Self-expansion during play. We have examined why people like play; the rewards of play are the reason we invest energy in it. Behind the accompanying, and frequent, Self-expansion is that – as the new cognitive schemata are established from existing information, and children lack many basic level connections – children find connections easily when playing. Without realization during play, most cognitive schemata would not be established. We would then have a great deal of encyclopedic – but little usable – knowledge. Another major point is that play is a model of reality which does not contain the inconveniences – in military games, death and injury; in medical games, pain and illness – so the profit is disproportionately large compared with the investment. There are virtually no inconvenient episodes, but the great number of realizations causes a great deal of Self-expansion.

This raises the question of why do we not play until the end of our lives? Because play only models the outside world. We manipulate the outside world on a high level in vain; it remains a model. It does not matter if we always win at "Monopoly", our personal wealth remains the same. If the play-acting is of an exceptional model of reality, it can be a small step to matching it to the real world. This in turn raises the question of personality, principally in connection with our response to stress. As an example, what are our feelings when we begin to play poker with stakes of real money, rather than with matches or tokens?

One difference between play and work is that, at work, we no longer manipulate the models of mental representations, but the representations themselves, so our actions are irreversible.

Principal points covered in this chapter:
- 'reality'
- hierarchies of schemata
- children learning through play

When in a tale the grandfather bear meets grandmother bear, he understands that his grandparents are married. Moreover, he realizes that, generally, there is a mother next to a father, and that usually they are married

11. THE MENTAL HYGIENE EFFECT OF A COMMON RELIGIOUS ACT

Confession as a mental antiseptic.

Confession

Confession seems a bizarre and illogical act for neutral observers: as an example, after I commit a murder, by simply telling somebody else of this my responsibility vanishes, and everything goes on as if nothing had happened. This happens on the level of a phenomenon, so agnostics or atheists can be rightfully suspicious that this is one more tool used by the church to extract information from its 'dependents'. However, confession is more complex than can be described at the level of a phenomenon. It is an internal, psychic process connected to the church emphasizing psychological functions before behavior.[219]

The theological background of confession in Catholic religion is that Man has always been born as a sinner; that was Adam and Eve's covenant with God when they ate the apple. This is seemingly unjust: what has the decision made by two people thousands of years ago to do with me, even if – as "everyone" comes from Adam and Eve – I admit my descent from them. This culpability is canceled by baptism, a chance given to us by God which, if taken, enables us to stand with a clean slate (soul) before God. Therefore, baptized children do not have sins. Moreover, as it is intention that counts, as long as the child does not purposefully perform an evil act, he cannot sin.

However, as soon as the child begins to make conscious decisions about his acts, he can be in one of two conditions: sinner or sinless. Sinners go to hell when they die, the sinless go to heaven. So far, it seems clear. Then, what happens when someone sins? Religious or otherwise, the sinner experiences compunction. Psychologists have various explanations for this:

o some interpret it as a result of learning: generally, sin is followed by punishment – beating, scolding etc. – and the effect of anticipating that is compunction;

o some link it to social education, and emphasize its evolutionary benefit, in that it deters us from further sin; and

o according to the Freudian approach, the complete function of psyche is based on the super-ego, which is there to keep the norms and fight with the ego – which sometimes misbehaves – because the id which represents our instincts makes it do so. Compunction is a by-product of this fight.

---

[219] focusing on what happens in the soul, instead of what happens in the visible, physical world

It is certain that, if somebody becomes weak and does not change the Self-expanded option, then he becomes Self-narrowed: he is anxious about the consequences of his act, afraid of its coming to light, and in general he feels bad. The main problem with the Self-narrowing called compunction is that – thanks to the function of human memory – it never ends. It fades with time but repeatedly returns, and can also exert effects that cause illness. If anxiety escalates, it can become permanent, and hinder attainment of mental balance. In "Crime and Punishment", Dostoevsky described how sin can even lead to suicide, more or less genuinely but, above all, suggestively.

Catholicism answers this with its theology, or in the guise of theology. It is a historic 'given' that priests are not ordinary men; they have a unique relationship with God following their ordination, and vow that they are his servant. This means nothing other than the opening of a communications channel to God; anything related in the confessional is told directly to God. Since they are only a channel of communication in this role, they have no right to retain, talk about, or imply anything to do with this information. That is the so-called "Seal of Confession", the priest-penitent privilege that is recognized by the laws of many countries. In other words, the priest cannot pass on whatever he has heard in the confessional[220] as it is not himself who is being told or informed to, but the Lord. Since the Lord cannot answer directly, the priests answer for him; according to Catholicism, the Lord suggests the answer to the priest.

Therefore, it may be that someone hurts somebody else by thinking selfishly and finding a Self-narrowing solution to a problem; for example, he is short of cash, and so steals a wallet. A tension then arises in him, which might remain with him until his death, even if he returns the wallet and money, as certain (negative) elements become embedded in his Self, which narrow it. He goes to the confessional, which guarantees complete anonymity, and he relates his act to the servant of God.

What happens in the confessional from a psychological viewpoint? Somebody shares a secret and relives an event. Sharing a secret decreases the tension (Self-narrowing) caused by the secret, according to how many people we tell and to whom we tell it.[221] If I tell a secret only to my wife and my best friend,[222] it will barely decrease the tension, as there are virtually no consequences. If I tell the police it might have serious consequences, as the police represent society; in effect, I tell everyone. In many instances, the police are not interested in the issue, or analyze it only on the levels of the scale of the act, and the physical reality of its consequences. It is not their duty to deal with psychological motives. However, sharing the secret with a priest is perfect, in that I share my secret with "the universe", who will understand it in the way I want it to be understood. God only listens to me, and theoretically 'reads my thoughts'; we need not go into detail and bother

---

[220] the small box-like construction with two doors to two compartments separated by a grid, in which people can be heard, but not seen or identified visually, by the priest
[221] how important those people are
[222] who will not hurt or betray me

with protracted questioning and answering; a 'perfect' communication takes place. Psychologically, the guilty person has the experience of saying those words used to share the secret; he has to say "I stole the wallet". However, it only matters to him, as God is "all knowing"; he knows that the guilty person stole the wallet, the reason why, and what it meant to him. As well as sharing, the key is reliving.

The effect of words is often surprising, as when we put something into words, or digitize analogous information.[223] During this process the information is involuntarily restructured, and a new cognitive schema emerges which, until that point, was merely a set of acts and sensations with an emotional tone.[224]

The next most important aspect is so-called 'sincere regret'. Namely, that it is not enough to say automatically "I stole a wallet", but we have to experience the negative nature of the event and plan how to avoid making the same mistake again. The whole story happens between the person and God: no one[225] knows what sin encumbers the soul of that person. Nevertheless, even the priest cannot determine whether the person does or does not regret what he did. Moreover, it is not the priest's duty to judge this. As nobody can call him to account, everyone understands that confession only serves to make the penitent feel – or seek to become – better.

There are two further aspects related to confession:

Penitence: the so-called penitence (remorse) levied on the sinner by God,[226] is nothing more than a certain amount of prayer, in proportion to the weight of the sin(s).[227] It is not difficult to admit – or see – that this is a strictly symbolic form of compensation – a mere five to ten minutes of prayer – to relieve oneself of the sins. However, this 'compensation' is compulsory. Because of its meditative nature, prayer has the effect of preparing one for the end of the phase of Self-narrowing. In a Self-expanded state, prayer helps inner communication and the absorption of inner processes required for remorse.[228]

Remission (communion): within the sacred framework of the mass, one of the high points is the repeating of the last words of Jesus at the Last Supper, when he blessed the bread and wine. So Jesus's body becomes identical with the bread, as does his blood with the wine. During communion, a person has a piece of holy bread[229] placed in his mouth, which is a piece of the body of Jesus, so he becomes one with him. The communion is bi-directional:

o as the communion can take place between two similarly sin-less entities, only those whose souls are without sin might become one with God; either they

---

[223] words store information in digital format, while our emotions are stored analogously

[224] he had had the opportunity to talk to himself about stealing the wallet, but the final form of the cognitive schema emerges only by writing it down or telling it to somebody

[225] apart from the priest

[226] and communicated in words by the priest

[227] according to God's judgment

[228] because one achieves inner harmony with himself during prayer, he can more easily focus on himself, and his decisions can then touch higher-level cognitive schemata. The relaxed state of Self-expansion then helps the restructuring of his cognitive schemata, which is required to change bad habits

[229] a flat wafer of bread, the host

confessed recently[230] or had not committed serious sins since the last confession. If you want to take part fully in the most holy event of the mass, to relive the communion with Jesus, you should cleanse your soul by confession

o the communion, on the level of an individual, is the last step of the confession/penitence process towards obtaining God's forgiveness.

The act of communion[231] is the turning point towards Self-expansion. As the wafer-thin host disintegrates in the mouth of the person, the possibility of a new life opens, by being able to begin again everyday life without sin.[232]

The Catholic Church is often presented as authoritarian, which is true from many viewpoints. However, as with most religions, the Catholic Church was established principally to conserve the essence of the religion and to survive. The service of confession in its churches is considerably liberal and democratic, and it respects – and builds upon – the function of psyche. Why is this so? The confession/communion is on one hand a mental antiseptic.[233] This can preserve the mental balance of the morally frail, and easily sinning people, who could break down if confessing to serious sins, even if they still have the strength to change to the 'right' way. The first step in using the opportunity of confession is to accept that there is a higher entity that has power over us. It cannot work without this. If someone is so Self-narrowed (evil) that he is incapable of uniting with his Environment by Self-expansion, he will not go to confession in the first place. It is hard to imagine Stalin or Hitler, while sending millions to death, rushing to priests to confess.

In addition, excessive Self-expansion does not allow confession: if my Self is so big that I feel that I am a king, and everyone must serve me, then I will not accept someone to mediate between me and God. I will want to talk to him directly, not through a priest. That is why I cannot imagine that Napoleon or Elvis would go to confession. Someone has to be in a normal state to start on this path: neither too Self-narrowed[234] nor too Self-expanded (contemptuous).

However, the abovementioned conditions are not exclusive. The opportunity is open, even for the greatest murderers, to return to the righteous path, and be able to attain Self-expansion again. The church, or Jesus, laid the decision of trying to return to the righteous path in the hands of the individual. To illustrate this, consider that there are no control points for outsiders: nobody can control a mass-murderer's internal (soul) processes. If someone only simulates the whole process and meanwhile thinks about how he will cheat on his wife, then he will be no different from someone who genuinely regretted their sins and who will be a better (more Self-expanded) person the next day onwards. This notwithstanding that he

---

[230] so all their sins were forgiven and so their souls were thereby cleansed
[231] the priest placing the 'body' of Jesus in the mouth of the person
[232] assuming that he genuinely regretted his sins and carried out the act of penitence
[233] preventing mental illnesses, fighting against anxiety, and soul distorting effects
[234] in religious terms, he "has lost his connection with God"

may speak in the confessional in exactly the same way, kneel in prayer,[235] and take the host in his mouth.

This being without control delegates the decision to the deepest part of the person. We have to square our conscience with nobody else, so usually most people would rather not go to confession than attend and apparently confess, but not genuinely.

These Self-repair mechanisms work not only on an individual level; they also affect communities. During confession, people will, more or less, commit themselves to changing their bad habits, and to try to take decisions so that their Self will remain/become expanded.[236] This approach also has a positive effect on those people who do not believe, or who do not attend confession, in two ways:

o those who confessed after re-evaluating their existing relationships are given the chance to repair, in reality, their broken relationships; they get rid of negative feelings towards their enemies.[237] So, either they are given one more chance to turn a bad relationship into a good one, or they can start to reverse the effect of their sins in real life;[238] and

o there is a psychological effect associated with that new chance. When you have one (theoretically last) chance to be good again, you try harder to be good. This is like a child who becomes extremely dirty whilst playing. After a while he becomes disturbed by the mud and dirt. He takes a shower,[239] puts on clean clothes, and so experiences how good it is to be clean. Then he will try harder to keep himself clean when he goes playing again.

Before assuming that I have an overly idealistic opinion of confession, I must note its limitations. These arise from:

o the human nature of the sidemen;[240]
o the innate insincerity of people;[241] and
o the aims of the church as an institution.[242]

Apart from these limitations, I believe that confession is a fortunate and useful institution, which has probably saved the mental health of millions of people,[243] and improved mankind. However, the intention of this detour was not to make a judgment, but to demonstrate a psychological phenomenon that is interesting from the viewpoint of our FIPP model.

Finally: in Judaism, forgiveness and regret are not connected to the mass, but to a celebration (Yom Kippur) when everybody apologizes to God for the sins they have committed against others, and forgives those who have sinned against themselves. At the same time, everybody apologizes to everyone they know, and every-

---

[235] whether he prays in the meantime, or thinks about the next atrocity, is something nobody else will know
[236] for example, helping others; behaving in an unselfish way; avoiding the use of aggression
[237] the obligation to forgive your enemies is a part of the confession
[238] this obligation is also a part of the confession, more exactly, the penitence
[239] which he may normally loathe
[240] priests, who can pray on the Seal of Confession
[241] for example, people in small communities may confess only because of peer pressure
[242] an example being the influence exerted by priests upon all strata of society throughout the ages
[243] consider adolescents who experienced continual compunction due to their increased sexual interest

body has to forgive everybody who apologizes to them.

Principal point covered in this chapter:
- the psychology and redemptive nature of confession

12.   THE DIFFERENT PATHS TO HAPPINESS

Can 'happiness' be described? * And then we die; views using FIPP. * Freedom = Self-expansion...or selfishness and Self-narrowing? * Pursuing Enlightenment? * Sex without end is not an answer. * Religiosity as Self-expansion. * Buddhism, Judaism, Christianity, Nirvana. * Happiness through subjective performance. * Altruism can expand and narrow the Self. * The psychology of invention. * Maternal Self-expansion. * The blinkers of competition. * Travel; to or from Self-expansion? * Acquiring knowledge; 'reading' forming cognitive schema. * Arts patronage. * FIPP and post-death existence. * The moment of death and fast-forwarding flashbacks.

About happiness

Despite the historical search for a definition of happiness, psychology today talks, at most, about happy people within the concept of mental health. The connection between happiness and mental health is quite strong, but happiness – and the ways of reaching it – has not become a part of mainstream research, although it has been discussed in positive psychology.[244] This is due to many reasons:
   o as a concept difficult to define, representatives of science are not too eager to deal with it;
   o as a concept that embraces the totality of human life, it is seen as more in the territory of philosophy;[245]
   o it greatly overlaps with religion, which does not deal with the study of happiness,[246] but the question of a "good life" (from different viewpoints) is at the center of their interest. In addition, the logic of religion is directly opposed to the logic of science.[247]
Despite these reasons, it seems clear that it would profit mankind if science provided some guidance on how to attain happiness, which would also state something of the meaning of human life.

The presented model – Fodormik's Integrated Paradigm for Psychology (FIPP) – enables us to understand joy and happiness from a cognitive point of view. We have seen that FIPP describes thinking processes in problem solving. It can also

---

[244] for example, Seligman, Csikszentmihalyi etc.
[245] cf. life philosophies
[246] because they examine our relationship with transcendence
[247] as they do not prove, but simply accept, things in which one 'has' to believe

say something about sexual life and gender differences. Since FIPP is rooted in system theory, it is worth examining further, whether the patterns it describes also work in relation to other systems.

As an example, a society is a system, but so are the human brain, groups, companies, and the family. It is, therefore, not illogical that, if we look for the same pattern in these systems, that how we perceive things is simply a matter of organization and viewpoint. It is about the same people, just that at one time we consider them as elements that assist a company, another time as units of race-preservation (family), and yet another time as parts of a community bordered by geographical borders. "Reality" is the same, the only difference being the viewpoint, the way we model reality, and at what level we observe.[248]

In examining the topics of smoking (a spliff) and sex, we observed certain isolated parts of human life. In attempting to apply FIPP to all of human life, the aim is to define happiness, and compare ways that lead to it.

Initially, we must learn something of, what is for many, an unhappy event: the end of our lives.

FIPP and death

We initially tested FIPP with problem solving. But happiness is connected with life, not problems. Or would life then be a problem as well? If it was, how can we be so different and yet still have common problems? Is there also a turning point in life, when something new emerges, such as a new cognitive schema emerging during the process of problem solving?

Probably, yes. Our common problem is that we are going to die. Since we were born, so we will die. It is an axiom, based upon the biological nature of human existence, that we need to do something about our own (physical) dissolution.

If the problem is "how do I deal with my death?", then how is happiness connected to it? To answer this, we must temporarily divide the concept of happiness into short-term[249] and permanent happiness. In discussing permanent happiness, we touched upon solving the problem of "what can I do about my death?" That is, about accepting death as the natural order of life, that our physical presence is a temporary condition which goes against the normal flow of the universe. What is meant by 'going against the normal flow of the universe'?

---

[248] just as a tree is part of a forest, and the forest as a mass of trees is the same thing on a different level, so applying FIPP on different levels sheds light upon different things

[249] we can call it joy; for example when seeing a person for the first time in ages

Death and the laws of nature

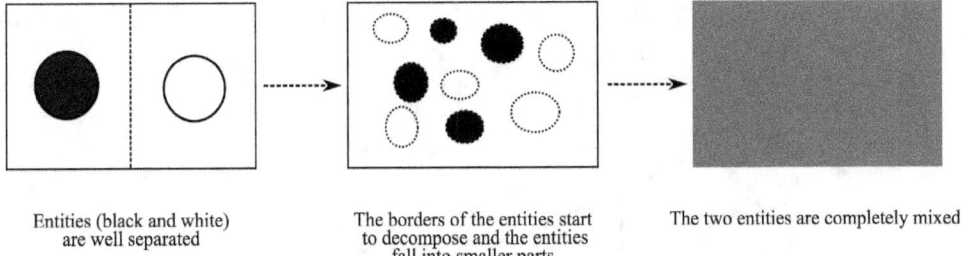

| Entities (black and white) are well separated | The borders of the entities start to decompose and the entities fall into smaller parts | The two entities are completely mixed |

Figure 56: A system's different stages as entropy increases

One of the most general of physical laws is the so-called principle of growing entropy; the alternative name is the Second Law of Thermodynamics. The concept of entropy shows how inordinate a system is: how evenly the elements and energy of a system are distributed. In other words, how the distribution of the elements of the system is very similar to random distribution.

The principle of growing entropy says that a system strives to be entropic, and that order is an unnatural condition of nature. So maintaining order[250] requires effort. Based on the concept used in the chapter on aggression, we can say that repulsive connection is against the laws of nature. We have also seen that boundaries are nothing but repulsive connections. If borders are against the laws of nature, then the splitting up of borders accords with the laws of nature.

The human body is an entity that has borders. Moreover, the Self has borders too, and people want to strengthen these borders. Nature inevitably handles this by using the principle of growing entropy as a temporary state: atoms manage to congregate against the principle of growing entropy for a while (cf. body) then nature wins and atoms begin to depart from each other (cf. decomposing body).

What people need to realize to accept their unavoidable death is that all their boundaries are temporary. They can only be maintained by force, and that it is normal that they will end. We do not have to separate ourselves from nature and society and their laws; we do not have to strengthen our separation from them; but we have to obey them. The meaning of obedience to these laws and flow, and whether we impersonate them, is now examined.

FIPP and happiness

For someone trying to apply the description of FIPP and its examples to himself whilst reading them, it will not be of any surprise if I say that the experience of Self-expansion is closely related to the everyday use of the concept of happiness.

---

[250] for example, keeping two things separated from each other

Perhaps even more than closely related, as there is the matter of pride at being a part of it, due to the enhanced Self and new competencies. This is the small difference that highlights why it is important to enter the new concept of Self-expansion within the formulation of FIPP. It is also the reason why I did not use the word happiness instead of the term Self-expansion.

However, with the help of FIPP, we can define happiness as experiencing Self-expansion.

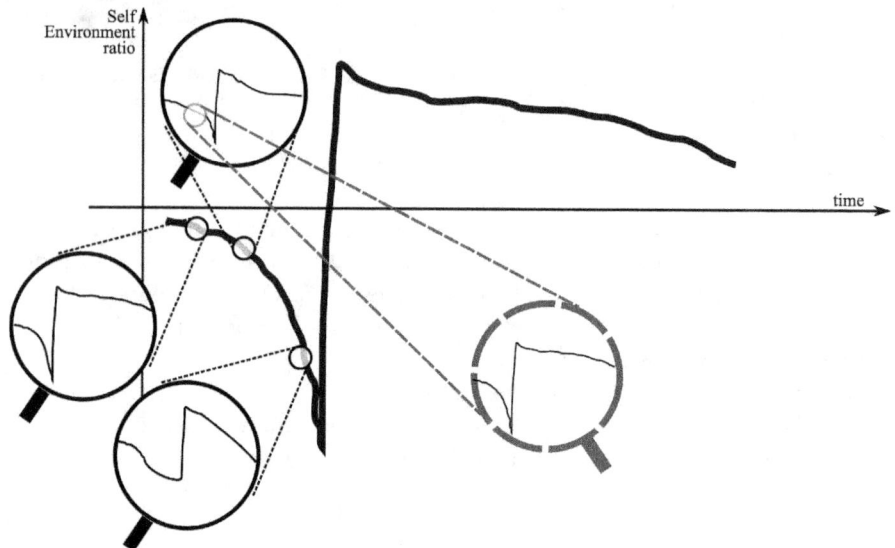

Figure 57: The FIPP-pattern used on different magnitudes of a process

I previously noted that, when examining happiness, we must keep the aspect of time within view: happiness is either manifested for a short time,[251] or is manifested as an elongated period (as a mental state). This division does not invalidate the previous definition (happiness = experiencing Self-expansion), as by being able to apply FIPP model at different levels and different complexities of phenomena also enables it to describe matters concerning different temporal courses. For example, when someone understands how to furnish his room,[252] then the new concept[253] is, in itself, the solving of a problem. However, during the execution, new partial problems occur.[254] On the level of schemata, these partial problems are the 'children' schemata of the concept, established by deduction from higher-level schemata. But these partial problems can include other problems as well.[255] The

---

[251]   so to say, as an impulse
[252]   or his office, his workbench, his computer's file system
[253]   a collection of ordering principles
[254]   I cannot connect two cables, a cabinet does not fit, etc.
[255]   the two cables can finally be connected, but the socket of one of them is slightly deformed; finally there is space for the cabinet, but it is not level

solving of such 'partial-partial-problems' also shows the FIPP-pattern, as it did with the discovery of the concept. So, it causes Self-expansion as well, which is equal to many small pleasures.[256]

As previously seen, schemata do not only have constituent parts (children schemata), but they themselves are parts of something. Together with other schemata, they make a higher-level schema. In our case, the room we furnished with our concept serves our comfort, improves our efficiency, and altogether enables us to achieve our goals. Thus, they contribute to a happiness that manifests itself over the longer term. If we continue the list, we can find what is common in the nature of pleasure and happiness: since achieving our goals, being better at our jobs eventually helps us to reach the final goal of life and contributes to whether, overall, we live a happy life or not.

The only question remaining is: what possibilities do we have in determining the final goal of our lives? Before answering, we should examine whether there has to be a final goal in life at all. Do we overcomplicate matters, or place an unnecessary load on ourselves by setting goals? Because it can also be – and this leads us to the question of freedom – that the goal hinders us.[257]

Freedom

Western cultures have been determined over the ages by the question:[258] which one is more important, freedom or happiness? From the moment we commit to something, we are no longer free.[259] This something can also be the final goal. So, if we have a goal, we cannot do anything and everything we want to any more; we are no longer free. The inverse of this logic follows: we should not have goals, so that we can preserve our freedom.

From another viewpoint, people who lack the competency of controlling the Environment are not free. Since the Environment controls them, they cannot do what they want to, and so they are not free.

Translating these thoughts into the language of FIPP:

"if we have a goal...we are not free" means that, as soon as we set a target or goal (an Environment), our commitment to that causes our Self to begin to narrow. Accordingly, is not being free the same as being Self-narrowed?

If we cannot control our Environment, then our Self is smaller than the Environment, so we are Self-narrowed. Do we reach the same conclusion, that the lack of freedom is Self-narrowing?

From all of this (if the Self-narrowed state is due to the missing freedom) we can draw the conclusion that the Self-expanded state is nothing other than freedom. This is supported by a visual example: birds are the symbol of freedom in

---

[256] pleasure as short-term happiness
[257] as an example of the hindering nature of goals, if my goal is to lose weight, then I cannot eat whatever and however much I want
[258] for example, existentialism, Sartre et al
[259] if we ever were

many cultures, as living in the air enables movement in all three dimensions. If we imagine the Self of a bird in the air, it is without boundaries, just like the air, since wherever there is air it can fly.[260]

The relationship of freedom and happiness

Is it not contradictory to first say that Self-expansion is happiness, and then that it is freedom? Moreover, we have also stated that these two are incompatible...

The free person loses his freedom and becomes happy when he finds the goal that suits him. While he works on achieving his goal, he advances the Self-expansion which will come to him, and which can also make him happy. Although it is possible that he endures a deal of frustration on the way to the goal, knowing he is on the right way makes him happy. That is, if he knows. While approaching the goal, when we meet difficulties we become uncertain whether we are really on the right path, and whether we really want that goal.[261]

If we do not commit to anything, in order to selfishly preserve our freedom, paradoxically our freedom loses its value. In other words, the value of freedom manifests itself when we give it up; until that point, it is seemingly worthless. Let us again look at birds. Try not to imagine an 'average' bird, but rather one which strives for absolute freedom that it wants to preserve forever; its ability to fly in all directions. If it starts flying in one direction,[262] a hillside will eventually be in its way. At this point, it might turn back to where it still has space; that may be the exact place where it came from. The more it fears its freedom, the faster it will turn back, until it will go around in circles. Sooner or later, it will starve in the air. However, despite freedom being important to the bird, it will not discover an exit from the valley through which he could have flown out.[263]

To summarize...if we do not commit to and do not choose an aim, although freedom remains, the lack of a goal will also result in never reaching anything new or attaining new competencies. Not having a goal, not struggling to reach a goal, keeps us from losing our freedom. If you do not choose a goal simply to stay Self-expanded – to be free – you miss the opportunity to further expand your Self by choosing a goal and reaching it.[264]

Enlightenment as a goal

According to FIPP, enlightenment is the condition in which we reach the final and maximum extent of our Selves. In the chapter on enlightenment, we described in detail that it is not attainable by everybody: our innate abilities play an important role in whether it is possible that a schema emerges that integrates everything.

---

[260] note that a bird, by its ability to fly, can control the air – the Environment – around itself

[261] for example, when sportsmen train daily to win the Olympics, which occur just once every four years, and have to daily persuade themselves that it is a goal worth working hard for

[262] for example, horizontally in a valley

[263] in psychological terms, it is afraid of exploration

[264] this Self-expansion is greater even than that which comes from freedom

Therefore, although in many cultures it appears black-and-white that there is a final goal, dangling enlightenment before the general public is futile. On the other hand, enlightenment is not something that can be forced. It is possible to develop in certain fields, which may establish a one-level-higher schema, and connect the well-known fields with others, but we cannot really want it. My belief in this is supported by the act of wanting something, which is a Self-narrowing procedure: that is, the concentration upon something. Also, enlightenment requires giving up the boundaries of the Self or, as previously mentioned, it requires admitting that we are controlled by laws and cannot counteract them. Perhaps enlightenment requires a combination of knowledge and humility. Here, humility is taken to mean: no longer wishing to increase the size of our Selves; not to think of the boundaries of our Selves as important; and, that that differentiating ourselves from the Environment is not important.

Objects of life: which path to enlightenment?

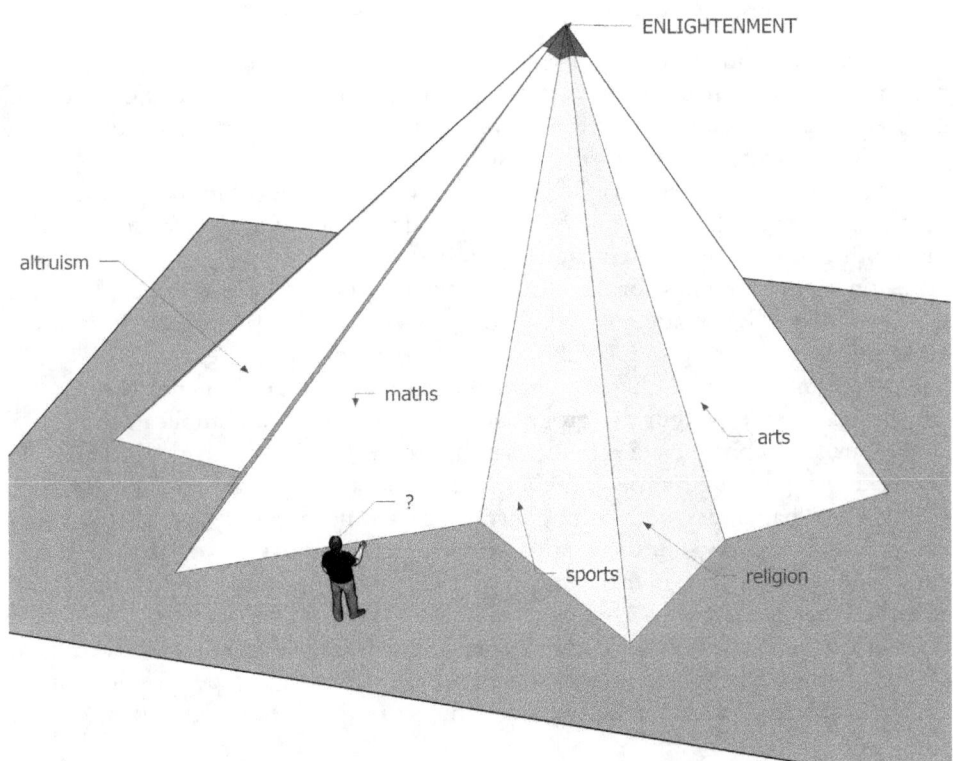

Figure 58: Different paths to reach enlightenment (the top of the mountain)

Following this speculation on freedom, we can exclude freedom as a purpose of our lives, as we must choose a goal for ourselves. Furthermore, we have seen instances of enlightenment as, initially, an overly aspirational goal. Let us, therefore, now review what other truly satisfying objects of life are available to people which can bring us closer to enlightenment and a happy conclusion of our lives.

There is a commonplace answer to the question in the title ("Which path to enlightenment?"): "So many people, so many ways"; but that is only partly true![265]. Just as a mountain can be climbed from different directions, so there are different ways of obtaining happiness. Though we can draw an endless number of paths on the mountain, the mountain has sides. Similarly, the pathways to happiness belong together according to their nature: we can distinguish religion, science, art, and society, as the main areas that help us to prosper in life.

It has been known since Freud that people's thinking is saturated with sex. It is also not a new discovery that the main goal of sex is pleasure. This seems, therefore, the first topic that we should examine closely.

Happiness by endless sex

If people were animals, the sole object of their lives[266] would be to give their genetic material to as many successors as possible. If it is a male, he should spread his seed indiscriminately, and fertilize until he is exhausted. Females should choose the healthiest male, and give birth to a successor every year.

So far, that is the oversimplified, lay interpretation of evolution. A little more complicated, but still a particularly biological definition of the purpose of life, is that both genders strive to ensure that their successors survive, and so pass their genes on with the highest probability.[267] Since resources are limited, people would have to hinder the spreading of competing genes, and give preference to relatives. So aggression towards others (and the successors of others) appears.

That evolutionary fact, that the chance of survival of certain genes is greater if the individual stays within the group, makes the issue more complicated. Beyond simple sex and reproductive activity, man has to deal with a more a complex issue: his relationship with other people, society, and cooperation within it. Therefore, no path leads to happiness from mere generational and nurturing effects.

A distorted version – unsuccessfully implemented in society – of the aim inherent in biological drives, is the sex-centered lifestyle propagated by Mr. Heffner[268] and the hippy generation. Orgasm is Self-expansion, and it would be logical to make it permanent by promiscuity, thus reaching a state of happiness. Even if we disregard the ethics of thousands of years, we can see that people do not get 'stuck' in permanent sex, even without ethics, as orgasm is a Self-expansion that

---

[265]   as we have seen in Chapter 7 on Enlightenment
[266]   the pre-requisite of their happiness
[267]   cf. selfish gene theory
[268]   founder of Playboy magazine

runs down quite quickly. As we experience the larger and longer Self-expansion of, for example, creation, a permanent state of orgasm will not seem to be particularly attractive as an object of life.

In activities that society respects at different levels, the height of those levels is in direct proportion to the strength and longevity of Self-expansion. And, fortunately, everything is in its place: the higher the level of the activity, the more social value it carries as it affects more people. For example, practicing science or building a house is incomparably more valuable to mankind than any purposeless sexual act.

Perhaps there is one stance that does not support the notion that the higher the level the act is, the greater its value and the Self-expansion it causes, and that is Buddhism. From a European perspective, the pursuit of Buddhism seems more selfish than socially valuable, despite it being seen as, notionally, a religion of a 'higher' level. This is because Buddhism only focuses on the individual by making the increase of Self-expansion the goal, not just a by-product. And this Self-expansion occurs – in one way or another – by disregarding social activities as by-products.

Another socially more valuable, but still sex-related topic, is the question of successors. Those who are childless will not have experienced that children can be the source of enormous Self-expansion, but that they can also cause many Self-narrowings. Watching our children causes Self-expansion. But the road to it is evidently not a series of Self-expansions. Childbirth is the transcendent event for many people; it causes huge Self-expansion.[269] But it is a temporary, not a permanent, condition.

The foregoing demonstrates that sex and creating children do not of themselves lead to happiness. We can ascertain that these basic connections[270] are deeply encoded in people, and provide an intense drive for them. We can also state that, the smaller the chance someone has of reaching a higher-level Self-expansion, the more he focuses on those Self-expansions that are biologically available to everyone.

Happiness in religion

Let us move on to the "mountainside", the closest relationship with Self-expansion itself: religion.

Not having seen the birth of the great religions, we cannot state the reason why they were established. If we think in a particularly material way (and accept the model of FIPP), we can imagine the situation as follows. People lived their lives and had Self-expansions as and when they realized certain successes. They began to name these phenomena that were connected with Self-expansion, talked about them with each other, until finally they felt they had to attribute these strange feelings to something. That was probably the time when the concept of transcen-

---

[269] without this, would women face the serious difficulties, and endure the pain, of giving birth?

[270] according to which, sex leads to Self-expansion, as does having a child

dence, or gods as the source of Self-expansion, was established. They could explain the event of Self-expansion only by assuming that there is something, beyond the physical realm, with which they were connected.

According to Judao-Christian religiosity, man consists of two parts: the divine part (the soul) and the physical part (the body). We can see changes in the physical during life. Of the mental part, we experience the phenomena called Self-expansion and Self-narrowing.[271] We can look on all of this from an inverted, cause-and-effect viewpoint, as religion teaches it. The Lord gave us the ability of Self-expansion (for example, we can pray), so that we can experience our divine part, and do not forget or ignore it. One way or another, Self-expansion connects with the transcendent, paralleling the process during Self-expansion when our Selves merge with the Environment, the world itself.

A teacher once stated that religions were born only in places where there were mountains. His explanation for this: that there is something about mountains that urges people to engage in transcendence.

I believe it is something else. If someone climbs a mountain, the scene in front of his eyes is a vast Environment, which he can also experience as a whole (nature) of which he is a part. For example, if he climbs to a familiar place, the valley he looks down on is on harmony, and he is safe: when he looks down on his village or recognizes the lake in front of him, he will have Self-expansion. Of course, if he is hanging on by his fingernails to the edge of a rock, that will more likely cause Self-narrowing.

So, where there is a mountain that can be climbed, by looking around Self-expansion can be experienced and obtained. In addition, the new perspective can provide us with realizations of new connections, so enhancing this Self-expansion. With the help of this rare perspective, which puts things into a different context, and provides a better visual representation of the proportions of man and nature, it is then easier to imagine a god who sees everything from above.[272]

Buddhism

I shall begin with this religion as its declared aim is to reach a condition in which the soul achieves Nirvana, a state of permanent happiness. The road to that is Enlightenment, which can be reached with meditation, prayer, yoga etc. It wastes no time on gods and afterlife, but purposefully seeks to establish the top cognitive schema that can both explain the whole world and answer all questions.

That is a distillation. I do not profess to know the minutiae of Buddhism, but imagine that it 'attacks' from the physical side of the "mountain". So, Self-expansion can be exerted by auto-hypnosis and relaxation; followers of this religion become adept at these techniques. The body is complex, so its mysteries have to be revealed before we can control it. That requires huge energy, and a lot of

---

[271] if not practicing science, we could call the two phenomena Soul-expansion and Soul-narrowing also

[272] it is a characteristic of 'god' in almost every culture that he or she is somewhere above us

time.[273]

Buddhism emphasizes the importance of getting rid of desires (and thus borders; see the chapter on aggression). It seems to me that Nirvana is that place where people can rid themselves of desire, and thus have nothing bonding them to earthly things. How does this enter our picture? Why would reaching Nirvana, and ridding ourselves of desires, be good for us? Because every physical thing we desire can cause Self-narrowing, and that causes discomfort. We work for it until we attain it, we narrow our Selves to achieve it, and to make it a part of our Selves. Then, when it is actually ours, we begin to worry that we will lose it, and that leads to new Self-narrowing. Only at the moment of obtaining do we obtain pleasure, even if 'it' is repeatedly obtained.[274] There is no Self-expansion without Self-narrowing except when we rid ourselves of all desires and unify with the Universe; we reach Nirvana.[275]

Let us turn to the issue of economics as a variation of the route to happiness.

Children know that wealth is relative. According to our needs, we can feel in childhood that we are immensely rich with just marbles in our hands, or in adulthood even the twentieth million dollar may not be enough to assuage our quest for wealth. I translate this as: our Environment is determined by our Selves, the question is…what is important to us at a given moment: marbles or money? Environment tries to manipulate the Self,[276] and the Self does not have perfect control over what it considers to be the Environment.

There are then two extremes of feeling rich:

o we get everything we need
o we decrease our needs to zero.

Buddhism tends to the latter. I also tend to a decrease in our needs, to be happy about everything we obtain as a bonus for using our abilities.

Judaism

The principal concept of Judaism is that of one God, and this God gave the Torah[277] letter by letter; if we read it attentively and thoroughly, we can answer every question (in connection with society and behavior). Since these answers come from God, they have absolute validity, and can be considered as laws.[278]

The function of the laws and an everyday relationship with the Torah can be imagined as branches that are points of decision in a person's life.[279] The Torah

---

[273] cf. how much time is required to be able to perform yoga techniques at a 'professional' level

[274] for example, seeing our children day after day, or receiving our salary regularly each month

[275] although it is a big joy to have a wife, children, a house, we can never be calm, as we always have to be afraid of something in connection with them: our wife leaves us, children get sick or become lost, our house burns down…. Moreover we need new, more, better, bigger, dearer: houses, cars etc. It is conceivable that this hinders achieving a Self-expanded state

[276] this happens in advertisements, when items appear of which we have never thought before, or when an unnecessary 'essential' breaks into our field of vision

[277] its Christian equivalent is the Old Testament

[278] for example, "you shall not murder" is one of these absolute commands

[279] beginning from what to do when I wake up, how to behave towards my enemies etc.

and unwritten tradition is nothing other than a system of connections hidden in a limited amount of information. This helps us at these branches, from which we can obtain the right answer at every decision point.

Religious Jews live well if they make the right decisions. Of course, the Torah cannot be there at every single move they make, that is why there are superior commands (laws), which more or less successfully give the right answer to a particular situation.

Religious Jews believe that, if someone acts according to the laws, that he then acts according to the will of God, by which he, so to speak, unites with God. We could say that this is exaggerated: absolute belief in the laws makes people behave rather like hypnotized people, who blindly trust a hypnotist and follow his commands. Pleasure comes from the ability of following his orders and thus merging with him. In this case, the hypnotist is the most perfect thing: God. We do not have to think about what we want to do in a situation, but we have to understand what God told us precisely in order to be able to execute it. Knowing that someone who keeps to the laws of God is on the right track causes Self-expansion; the Self merges with the Environment, which is nothing other than God. The more successfully someone keeps the laws, as he becomes more used to them and understands their common essence, the more he begins to understand the "will" of God, and so unifies with him.

The methods of merging the individual and God are greatly emphasized in religion: this goal is supported by short prayers, which people are obliged to repeat at almost every event.[280] The role of prayer is to constantly remind people that everything is due to God. It is a type of auto-conditioning: people expand their Selves with a force voluntarily chosen every time to connect to the Jewish Environment that symbolizes God.

In Judaism, the power of the community plays an important role: whereas the laws and prayers regulate the relation to transcendence, this is real. The community plays the role of the social Environment, the place where people live their lives. Nursing the relationship with the religious Jewish community[281] establishes a connection that helps the merger of the Self and the social Environment. The interest in the connection is that it does not only have an effect on the present. By remembering, with the help of feasts and rituals, it provides the people with the feeling of being a part of a family/community with a glorious and long past, that many other people feel the same way, and that this connection is unconditional and exists regardless of our will (on a quasi-genetic basis). This dissolution in the past (in time) and in the world (in space) causes Self-expansion and, at the same time, it satisfies the need of defining our selves.[282]

Another important element of Judaism is continual learning: the deepest possible knowledge and interpretation of the Torah. Discovering the connection hidden

---

[280] waking, eating, traveling, etc.
[281] on Sabbath dinners, feasts, in the synagogue etc.
[282] our identity

in the text causes (like problem solving in general) Self-expansion. Moreover, it also means – since it is a divine text – that the connections of absolute laws about the relationship of God and people are revealed.

Christianity

Jesus (who himself had been raised according to Jewish laws) brought something new – compared with Judaism – in the sense that he directed the attention from the outer level[283] to the inner[284] processes. The change was that the priority of the acts were replaced by the equality of acts, thoughts and intentions. In tandem with this he made a new law (a top level schema): Matthew 19:19 – "Thou shalt love thy neighbor as thyself".

Jesus did not want to change the basic teaching of Judaism. However, he thought that caring too much about the laws focuses our attention on appearance too much, since the laws cannot do anything with the invisible, inner processes. The regulation of the act granted the harmonic functioning of the society and the unity of the nation for the Jewish people, so it fitted the aim perfectly. However, regulation on the level of thought directly affects the Self, so co-ordination of larger masses became possible.[285] The acts and the inner world are independent of each other, as action does not influence the size of the Self. Religious Jews act for the mental representation of their acts, not necessarily for the representations of the consequences[286].

Based on this, we can consider the teaching of Christ as Jesus commanded: be Self-expanded in decision-making situations. If you do so, you will unite with God (the Environment), or, as your Self expands, it can reach the condition of uniting with the Environment (go to heaven cf. Enlightenment).

Let us understand this sequence of ideas through an example. A person walking in front of you drops some money on the ground. What do you do?

o Judaism precisely controls the situation, saying word by word what has to be done. You have nothing to do but execute it. After doing it[287] you feel that you kept the command, you acted in accordance with the laws of the world, therefore you became closer to God (you experienced Self-expansion).

o Jesus does not give you a straight answer, even if he explains in a parable a mechanism that works in similar situations. He says (according to my interpretation): "Make your decisions in order to expand your Self!" This can mean many things:

- if you keep to the main teaching (so you love your neighbor who walks ahead of you as yourself) then you do what would make you happy: to get back what is yours. Pick it up and hand it over! Here, Self-expansion means: your Self unites

---

[283]   discernible, phenomenological
[284]   so to say, cognitive
[285]   cf. the spreading of Christianity, evangelization
[286]   for example, we can practice charity without feeling anything in common with the person we help, but we can experience the pleasure of fulfilling our obligation to practice charity
[287]   reluctantly, or with pleasure

with the person who walks ahead of you (who is your Environment at that moment) and you feel what he feels, so you will be happy too when he gets back what is his. Perhaps Jewish teaching provides a similar command;

- however, what if you have more information in connection with the situation? For example, you have a hunch that the person who walks ahead of you has stolen the money and, as others are hungry, it should be given to them. You take it and give it to the hungry, and say it was given by the bad man. It is not you who gave it to them, but the bad man. Here, Self-expansion postulates a bigger Environment: now, not only the people who walk ahead of you are a part of it (including him) but others too (the hungry). And in that Environment, you achieve harmony according to your best knowledge and regardless of your selfishness: you give it to those who need it more, but you do not 'profit' from it. You do not feel that you acted correctly because money was given to the hungry. No, you did not give the money; rather the evil person did. You just put things in their places in the Environment, which accidentally reached the 'wrong' place. You could also say that God obtained the money from the evil man's pocket, and then dropped it on the ground, so that you could give it to the hungry. It is important that, in the act of 'giving-harmony-to-the-environment', your Self retreats into the background, which then guarantees an unselfish, Self-expanded decision.

This 'giving-harmony-to-the-environment' phenomenon was mentioned in the introduction as laws; for example, helping the growth of entropy. The money was not distributed evenly (the rich had more, the hungry had less), and this was against the growth of entropy. In that the money reached the poor, the entropy of the money increased, thus events took place in unison with the laws of nature. Of course, this parallel between entropy and the distribution of money is rather optimistic. However, we can illustrate with such visual examples that there are laws of society and nature, which we can oppose only temporarily. Going against them (or more precisely 'wanting-to-go-against-them') hinders reaching happiness. In Judaism, it is declared, even more clearly, that the laws of God which had to be kept are, at the same time, the laws of nature. As in Buddhism, it is the disintegration of the desires, the dissolution of borders, that results in the final calming and unifying with nature.

Happiness by performance

A friend gave the following reason for withdrawing from the world, at the age of just 30, and to begin living an ascetic, religious life, despite his successes in everyday life: "Let's assume that I work to make enough money to be able to marry the kind of woman I want. So far so good. I buy a house and a car. I marry a beautiful woman and we have children. Then we will need a bigger house because the kids grow up, and a bigger car. I work to be able to buy those. I bought them. So what? My wife loses her youthful attraction after a few years, and the children leave the house...."

That is how a person without religion thinks. For him, only the results of the physical world are conceivable, as only those 'exist'. Since he is a man, giving birth to successors does not excite his curiosity that much. Fortunately, despite the many mistakes of this friend, there is something very true about his realization: life has to have a purpose, because performance in itself (for example, making money) does not lead to constant happiness. Take professional athletes: if a single outstanding performance caused satisfaction or happiness in the long run, then every Olympic champion and world champion would retire the day following that performance. And in everyday, economic life, anyone who earned their first 10 million USD would retire from their job.

So people have to have a purpose to their lives. Moreover, a purpose of itself is not enough: we have to make a story around it so that we can explain how we chose that exact aim and to provide a more precise framework for that aim. As an analogy of the expression "narrative" in philosophy, I call this personal narrative. These personal narratives might have the same structure as the religions, but we can create one of these narratives on our own.

Goals and personal narratives

Different types of self narrative are known by everyone. If we look at a newspaper stand, we can read celebrity news about people who are envied. Some of these people have nothing else to do than trying to figure out how to make their life happier. The emphasis in choosing the right way is on their talent and abilities. Common to every solution is their aim of merging with the Environment:

o either by way of religion;[288] or
o by their individual solutions.[289]

Let us take a closer look at these.

Altruism as an objective in life

Altruism would assuredly win any vote on the nicest human characteristic, at least according to our present value system. Its definition: doing something which serves the interests of an individual or a group, even if it is against our own interest. Its archetype is Mother Teresa, who helped so many in need that she was awarded the Nobel prize. At first sight, it seems inexplicable. Why would someone give anything to strangers, or dispense the money he or she gained through hard work? But it is evolutionarily reasonable. The chapter on altruism discusses in detail both the function and mechanism of altruism. For those who have not yet read that, a brief summary.

When we give money to a beggar, or otherwise help someone, we feel good about that. Psychology describes the phenomenon, but the explanation of the underlying process is not easy, as so far it can only be explained by empathy. According to this, we reward ourselves through seeing and experiencing the other

---

[288] Madonna and Kaballah, Richard Gere and Buddhism, Cruise and Travolta and Scientology
[289] Princess Diana and Bono through their charity work, Bill Gates with his charitable foundation and expenditure of billions of dollars

person's pleasure (relieved situation). According to FIPP, it is about dissolving the border of the Self, and so letting the Environment in and merging with it. We therefore act by looking at the common profile of the Self and the Environment. The merging of the Environment with the Self can be seen as Self-expansion. And it is known that Self-expansion provides a positive experience. The fact that this also happens according to the FIPP-pattern is supported by the deadlock before it, when we hesitate and consider before doing something against ourselves.[290]

Helping others[291] is a pro-social activity, but the efficiency of the execution is often questionable. Although the goal is pure, the way it is realized often takes matters in the wrong direction,[292] or cancels out the effort. That is why help does not have a top form that is the most valuable, but instead has many variations according with what is considered the most effective, and by whom. Who and how we can help also depends upon our Environment: the doctor who heals neighbors helps in one way, UN employees or charity people help in another, while voluntary helpers, dedicated politicians or government advisors help in others. There are people who teach in African villages, because that is what they can do, and there are people who are cavers or first-aiders who help at disaster areas.

It is common that the saved person, the healed patient, and the hungry, give an enormous experience to the people who help. However, it takes great naiveté not to notice that, besides this Self-expansion, there are a lot of irritating circumstances[293] which cause Self-narrowing to the helpers. Unfortunately, there will always be suffering in the world; the realization of this leads to mental exhaustion in many altruistic people. Since the fight against problems never stops, altruism of itself does not give us complete happiness, as it is like a drug: the more we help, the more we want to help, and the more trouble we see and experience.

Scientific research and artistic creation

Previously mentioned was that mankind can be helped on many levels, dependent upon the abilities of its people. A special case is of discoveries, inventions, arts, and sciences. I consider these matters special as, particularly if they are pursued by people of talent, they are all self-rewarding. The Self-expansion accompanying the establishment of a new cognitive schema can maintain creativity independently of any physical circumstances: for example, money; how many starving poets/painters/inventors, such as Van Gogh, have there been?

Constant creation, and sharing the new cognitive schemata, would theoretically be a good solution for finding a happy life, as discoveries and works of art help people to realize and understand the laws of the world. This helps us all to live in harmony with the world. However, this path is not given to everyone as a possibil-

---

[290] the archetypal story of such hesitation is when Jesus decided to die for the good of mankind. The dead point before that was his last night in the Garden of Gethsemane, when he had his last chance to escape. Instead, he waited for the soldiers to find him, despite knowing the suffering awaiting him

[291] supplying food to the hungry in Africa, caring for the sick etc.

[292] for example, the leader of a tribe takes all of the supplies; or unsuccessful surgery caused by malpractice

[293] stealing, mistakes, bad organization

ity, because some lack the required ability. Individual differences play an important role in the fields of personality, ability, and self-estimation. It does not matter if someone has wonderful images or thoughts in his head if they cannot be realized as his skills are all manual, or he cannot think rationally, or is too impatient to work out the details properly. Individual differences play an even bigger role in sharing the cognitive schemata, when personality can determine how much others accept his intellectual products,[294] or how he deals with the (often negative) reflection of the social Environment.

Moreover, doubt always accompanies creation, and doubt is Self-narrowing. Is what I have done nice? True? Correct? If it is, is it something new?[295] Could I have done the same thing better? These questions are the great enemies of artists and scientists. If someone is talented, and the age in which he lives understands him, his personality remains healthy and he reaches happiness on this path. That is why I believe it probable that Picasso or Einstein were happy.

Mental health and creation is not a simple issue. In particular art, and science, heal, if someone connects to reality through these, if for nothing other than the frequent Self-expansion obtained. This dissolves the tensions and contradictions between the cognitive schemata within the Self. However, the brains of very talented people are rarely coupled with competencies that enable living with 'average' people to be smooth. Even if they were, the growth of the Self, which subsists on research/creation, makes living together difficult.[296] It is not only a question of will and situation that might generate serious friction between the researcher/artist and his environment. He often pays for his talent with disadvantages in other fields. How can he assure harmonic, balanced development in all fields if there is a favorite field[297] as the strong attractive force? The pursuit of that field rewards him more than anything else does.[298]

Children and grandchildren

Women have a great advantage in achieving happiness: their ability to give birth, and what comes of that, their instinctive attraction to children. Moreover, society supports them in this activity, since there is no other group of people that would value investing so much in their successors. The fact that they are already halfway along the route designated by biology 'guarantees' them 50% happiness. Of course, personality plays a role here as well: are they capable of loving their child, do they build good relationships with them, do they practice good educational techniques?

However, guaranteed Self-expansion still remains for them, which they feel when

---

[294] think of the strange personality of Dali or Warhol, or those inventors with poor communicational skills or introverted personalities
[295] have I given mankind anything new by this?
[296] if some of the scientific or artistic community considers X as a unique talent, there is a chance that after a while X believes that helping his wife with the housework is a waste of time and beneath him
[297] that in which he is exceptionally talented
[298] it is hard to imagine that Einstein would have been happy to go to cookery classes if he had had the possibility to solve physics exercises instead

they look on the children playing, and later their grandchildren. They feel that their blood flows in their veins, and they experience the identical existence of them and the family, and it makes them happy. Of course, this is not eternal either, since children and grandchildren grow up, there are conflicts etc. Still, for many women, the path to happiness is nothing but the greatest possible number of children with the best possible upbringing and the connection with them; in other words the unity of family.

There is only one thing against the automatic happiness of women who are capable of giving birth and bringing up their children: unfortunately for them, there is also an animus within them that desires other kinds of pleasures as well.

Eternal competition – oil billionaires

America and Anglo-Saxon culture, does not, allow slacking: there is an underlying feeling that those who stop are lost. So what often happens is going to the extreme: forcing competition and constant fighting.

Multi-billionaire oil moguls were asked how they could be motivated to increase their wealth even further? We should understand that getting rich from oil did not require a special talent in 20th-century America, unlike, for example, the creation, building up, and management, of a multi-national corporation. Some fortunate people were in the right place at the right time, and fought others for control of oil fields, as happened in gold mining. So, oil moguls knew each other, and fought for their millions by competing with each other. It is not about the money in the long run: money is only a measure of their skill and success, like centimeters in long jumping.

Of course, measuring somebody's skills by their wealth is a tendency amongst those who cannot stop making money.
- o I believe that very rich people are:
- o either simply lucky, like lottery winners;[299] or
- o born competitors. That is not to say that their personalities are injured in some way, but it seems to be something similar. If someone cannot give up making money, and worries even after a certain level of fortune has been reached, it would seem that he is running from something:
- o because he is good at nothing else.[300] It makes him a specialist in a narrow field with no other interests, and he has a decreased chance of finding peace of mind;
- o or because he finds pleasure only in making money. His brain is constructed in such way that he can answer problems which come up in a particular market or industry, or he is a talented businessman, so he generates a constant aha experience by solving problems. From this viewpoint, it is similar to the category of the artist/scientist described earlier; or he is running from a

---

[299] for example, he establishes a firm, which stands on its own feet after a while, and makes a fortune. He keeps his shares but has nothing to do anymore

[300] whatever else he would do, the slower progress in that field would frustrate him, and his personality is not mature enough to deal with failure

problem.[301] He is successful in his work, and too lazy to struggle in other fields because he is not successful there, or that directly injures him; or he gives something to the world that is needed. And he is the only one who can provide that. Here, this person can be happy if he does not measure himself by the amount of money,[302] but in more human things: how many people his firm provides jobs for, how many people are happier every day for obtaining his products etc.

The problem with money and constant competition is that society supports this attitude, thus spawning very specialist people who are blinkered to other areas. Many societies demand altruism and contribution as opposites in a healthy way. Both direct the attention of rich people to others, and compensate society for the supposed loss that the rich obtain unjustly on a social level.[303] Obeying this pressure takes our 'poor' billionaire out of the treadmill of everyday life. An alternative contribution is when people who become rich engage in politics. This is, theoretically, another form of altruism (or should be) as it is a form of acting for the common good.

Travel: an escape from seeing the end

In biographies, we can find often travel as a hobby, and people who have had 'once-in-a-lifetime' experiences that took place during a journey. What was so unique about those journeys is a different issue: the quality of the accommodation and food, the adventures or the landscape, perhaps something to do with the people or culture. If someone wanted to learn about landscapes and the shape of nature, theoretically he would not now even have to leave his home. He could simply switch on the Travel Channel, or surf Google Earth. I can think of two reasons for travel that surrogates cannot easily substitute:
  o if someone feels bad in the culture where he lives and wants to move
  o if he needs to have new stimuli all of the time.

If someone travels to the same country,[304] for example, the Seychelles, and regularly, or obsessively looks for a place where he feels good, that is most often due to the structure of his brain not fitting in with the culture he lives in. If we believed in reincarnation, we could say, for example, that the soul of a person from the Seychelles is reborn in the body of that regular visitor, and that is why he returns again and again to the islands.

If we consider the time and energy spent on travel, we can see that people make serious efforts to obtain something in return. What is the pleasure or satisfaction provided by a journey? Every culture has a particular logic and a particular value system, similar to that we mentioned in connection with the brain: life[305] is organized differently in an Arabic country as compared with, say, German culture. How-

---

[301] it may be the wife, children, a problem in childhood etc.
[302] as in something which is independent from his Self, or which symbolizes only a part of him
[303] for example, money retained by avoiding taxes, profits from arms manufacturing or gambling etc.
[304] not considering travel due to sport or business
[305] time, space, human relationships etc.

ever, the way we look at the world, genetically or family-wise, and the order in which we feel good, is a faculty that does not necessarily fit the geographical territory someone was born in. For example, if somebody is slow because of his hormonal function and nervous system, but he was born in Manhattan, he feels much more at home in a slow, sleepy Mediterranean town, where nobody is in a hurry. The same applies to human relationships: if a direct, sociable person is born in a cold, Northern country, he will have a series of Self-expansions if he moves amongst people (for example, in Greece) who are happy with strangers and trust them without question. The opposite can be true as well: if a Greek person has more vulnerable self-boundaries, perhaps he would rather live in a place where nobody wants to interfere in his life, and people, in general, keep a greater distance (for example, London or Sweden).

In these cases, things naturally happen in a way convenient for the person who sees repeatedly that life can be lived differently (exactly the way he wants) from what he is used to; this will lead to unspoken and unconscious Self-expansions. All he feels is that everything is in its place. Which is of course untrue, as there is no culture that fits someone perfectly, but things will on the surface, work smoothly (what a tourist sees). When someone returns to a place regularly, it means that the matching of the person and the culture goes deeper than the surface.

The opposite of Self-expansion provided by engaging with the culture are the Self-narrowings we feel before the journey: packing, planning the route, the inconvenience that comes with travel itself.[306] Arriving and acclimatizing to a new place are signs of long-lasting Self-expansion. On these occasions we expand our minds almost compulsively at the beginning.[307] Then, after awhile, we expand our minds purposefully to embrace the new Environment (and we begin to adapt), for that is why we went there. The new stimuli inundate us, new cognitive schemata are established, people begin to understand the local culture at their own level, thus they are enlightened. We recognize items, styles, scenery we have seen on photographs fall into place,[308] and these all cause Self-expansion. Tourism from this point of view is a journey with Self-expansion: we jump from obviousness to obviousness, then we return home. That is why it is so horrible when something bad happens,[309] as that deters us from permanent Self-expansion.

Based on the above, it could be seen that travel is an artificial, Self-expansion which we purchased. This immediately raises the question: why do we spend money on travel? Staying at home means confronting our real lives, that we might live without goals. Moreover, and more frightening, is that we realize that our lives are meaningless. Collecting experiences endlessly during a journey is like collecting money: having more experiences or money does not enrich our personality. What is worse is that the experiences[310] are very difficult to share.[311] It does not matter

---

[306]   for example, waiting at the airport, long journeys etc.
[307]   for example, when we have to adapt to the local customs; in Italy, shops close during the afternoon
[308]   for example, Santorini in blue-and-white, Arabic calligraphy, Arabs in dressed in robes etc.
[309]   for example, someone is robbed or kidnapped etc.
[310]   cognitive schemata established during the journey

that I see a thousand different cultures. Besides some colorful stories and a few well-taken photographs, it is all mine. Still, Self-expansion is complete if we can share the new cognitive schemata.[312] What remains is returning home, a Self-narrowing period at home again, and the hope that we can hold on until the next trip.

One last argument for the illusory nature of this solution: did Einstein travel using the money earned from his work and awards? Was Mother Teresa excited when she traveled? Did Picasso need to spend holidays in exotic places? There are people who develop their interior world – and enrich themselves – by giving to others. Others try to steal the beauty of the world using their sight or camera, but it does not actually penetrate them. They will not be wiser or more open and, above all, they cannot give to others. Would we be happier if we gave to a poor family the price of a holiday to the Seychelles?

This is not to say that I dislike travel: I enjoy it. The difference I want to emphasize is that there is travel that enriches our personalities, and travel providing only short-term experiences that are quickly forgotten.

Endless acquisition of knowledge

We should differentiate the endless acquisition of knowledge into types:
o autotelic
o seemingly autotelic but engaged in God (see studying Torah in Judaism)
o integrative acquisition of knowledge with an aim of publication

There is seemingly an ethical aspect anticipating that only autotelic of the above list does not lead to true happiness, due to it not giving anything to anyone. Since we examined 'seemingly autotelic' in the section on Judaism, let us examine the other two.

Autotelic acquisition of knowledge

Due to its distinctly intellectual nature, reading is universally respected. Someone who constantly reads has a certain standing in European society,[313] meaning a general moral appreciation. We could say that until somebody reads he does not – perhaps cannot – hurt others. We usually consider reading as a neutral activity, since reading takes time away from something perhaps more useful. The same time could be used in helping others, or engaging in other pro-social activities. This positive judgment also stems from the fact that readers can, while socializing, flaunt both their education and being well-informed.

It may be a harsh judgment, but one who reads a great deal seems to do so only because nothing assembles to him: he is engaged in acquiring information, rather than engaging in actual understanding. That he could do by being selective with,

---

[311] although the photographic and video industries are built upon it
[312] cf. accounts of experiences, travel films
[313] perhaps this originates in its positive judgment by Judaism, where lifelong learning is one of the most valuable activities

and limiting the number of, his choice of books on a particular subject. Another motivation for chronic reading can be a strongly introverted nature: reading accompanies loneliness. There are no rules for propriety or dress, as only the person and the book are together. This gives great freedom, but also a good reason, or excuse, for avoiding people.

Many people, upon finishing a book or article, immediately forget what they have just read. Others are incapable of integrating what they read. Even more people read newspapers and books of poor or questionable quality; tabloid newspapers come to mind. Now the internet provides many alternatives to reading. Accordingly, it is understandable that the number of chronic readers is gradually reducing. This does not mean that we do not have to read, rather, that we should read in optimal quantities. We should more carefully select what we read, as integrating badly constructed cognitive schemata in our Selves harms us instead of educating or helping.

But why do people do nothing but read? Depending on the intellectual level, there are always books that have something new to say. Saying something new is nothing other than establishing new cognitive schemata, which cause Self-expansion. A lot of reading provides many Self-expansions. The act of reading itself is a sign of Self-expansion: an act performed openly in one's Environment in a relaxed state.

Reading with the purpose of integrating

People having good general abilities can reach a point in their self-knowledge where they accept that, by themselves, they cannot give anything new to mankind. They measure and accept the limits of their abilities (initially, creativity), and choose the path of utilizing their different and unique abilities: of integration, memory, attention to detail, organization etc. These are the people who make science work by their own arrangement of information, distilling it and so making a dialog between different theories. They are a good source of information for those too impatient to read all of the literature on a subject.

This activity can lead to happiness, as people can feel that they not only absorb, but also provide a service. As previously seen, such giving is one way to Self-expansion. Autotelic reading lacks this sharing of knowledge.

Arts (collecting, cultivating)

A more visible measure of unlimited wealth, and more intellectual than jewelry or gold, is the art collection. Before reviewing the psychology of collecting art, we should recall that the principal aim of art is to obtain Self-expansion; this is enlarged upon in the chapter on beauty and aesthetic quality. Let us begin with the general acceptance that looking at a painting causes Self-expansion. The better the painting (it is also how we define it), the greater Self-expansion it causes, and for more people. Using this principle, let us disregard the collections acquired as investments by wealthy people who value art only by price, not for its aesthetic qualities. Such people see art as a status symbol. Instead, let us focus on those who appreciate the aesthetics of art as an exemplary life form that should be available to all people.

These people are determined in their pursuit of a painting or its provenance, and feel satisfaction (Self-expansion) when they succeed. In this and everything else, there is no difference between passionate collectors, whether of stamps, baseball cards, china, matchbox labels etc. They all obtain Self-expansion from improving their collection.[314] On the other hand, as they appraise their paintings, so they discover new connections, or conduct research in order to find connections between different pieces.

We could ask, "So what?" Imagining somebody living their life amongst art of immeasurable value, in constant fear of it being stolen or damaged, and doing nothing but eat, sleep and look at his art, makes us feel that this cannot be fulfilled happiness. The world of art collectors is a sub-culture: they know each other, each other's collections, brag about their new acquisitions and disposals. They live and breathe art.

Still…so what? Some of these collectors[315] leave their collections to their children, so that they can obtain a form of the happiness which comes from raising children. That is what happens to the collections of the aristocracy: the Prince of Lichtenstein, the British royal family. The problem remains that there is no permanent bridge between the Self and the wider (social) Environment, therefore permanent (lasting) Self-expansion cannot occur. So, they open their collection to the general public, or give it to the state. They can then finally step out of the confined world of the Self, and open up to the world by unselfishly giving again. This smacks of altruism, another way to happiness.

Another method that can also make a (subjective) bridge towards others is to patronize art. A wealthy person patronizing an artist with whom he can identify aesthetically, practically buys a share of the artist's Self-expansion arising from the process of creation. When the painter creates a work of art that the patron likes, the patron rightly feels that he has participated in the creation, that it is also due to him that the world is enriched by that work of art. At such times, we can be surprised at the purposes money can serve. Somebody can contribute it to the creation of great works without any personal creativity or without touching a brush, and can have a share in the pleasure of its creation. It is not by accident that art historians maintain accurate records of patrons and customers of former ages as the financial driving forces of the world of painting.

Returning to the publicizing of collections, we can discover a "Catch-22" which applies to other forms of Self-expansion. What is it like when someone opens his collection to the public, and then takes it back for some reason? Or gives it to the state, then requests its return? This is unimaginable, but this bi-directional nature is what gives a bad taste to Self-expansion in general: when you tell a secret to some-

---

[314] "One of the 1934 etchings of Picasso was still missing, but now I have that too. Now it is a complete collection."

[315] perhaps motivated by economic/tax considerations

one in a very intimate moment, and cannot take it back when the relationship goes wrong. However, if you do not tell it, there will be no intimacy.

This calls attention to Self-expansion having to be irrational to allow things to happen which would not happen rationally. At the same time, irrationality enhances Self-expansion, even if it is not its essence. That is more akin to the dissolution of boundaries and obstacles, which make the merging of the Self and the Environment possible.

The question is: can the Self reset the original boundaries after the Self-expansion passes? To use the previous examples: I told a big secret and someone will be able to blackmail me; or, I gave my collection to the state, and I watch helplessly as they store my biggest treasure in damp and dusty places. What can I do at such times? The rational answer would be: a.) do not be irrational; b.) secure their return or silence legally; or c.) ensure you that cannot be harmed. For example, you may have been told a secret in return; you make a contract with the state, declaring what they can and cannot do with the collection. In most cases, spoken words are very difficult to take back, and performed acts are very difficult to undo.

This legal attitude to contracts etc. detracts from the beauty of the situation. They require a Self-narrowed condition,[316] and so are against Self-expansion. The same applies to marriage contracts. They are logical, and rational, but they carry the germ of distrust. What we have discussed so far is: that there is no complete self-sacrificing, that the Self cannot become completely one with the Environment, that there is no absolute trust, as there is no absolute truth. However, everybody strives for truth, and we need a condition in which we can forget about this. We realize that condition by forgetting that which we are not supposed to forget.

Summary: FIPP's contribution to existence after death

Discussing a happy life is a difficult task. We cannot make ourselves completely independent of the moral aspect, although principles based on general human motivation can be demonstrated. Briefly, we can feel happy on our death[317] if we feel we have given something to the world, and so are at peace with our Environment. We might say that our Self (especially the boundaries between the Self and our Environment) started to decompose even before our physical body. A man's Self can merge with the Environment, as after he dies his physical body will merge with his physical environment ("ashes to ashes, dust to dust").

Morality and science should be separated. However, if morality does intrude, that should not be disturbing. That is, in the sense described above, in that science does not contradict any major traditional system of thought: morality, religion, Kant's categorical imperative,[318] psychology's image of mental health.

---

[316] contracts require concentration, maneuvering requires guile
[317] because what else counts if not the last moment that lights up – or, admittedly, clouds – everything that has happened before
[318] do to others what you would like others to do to you

Another result is that we can reduce the behavior of Mother Teresa, Einstein, Picasso, and Bill Gates, to a common denominator. Everybody gives something to the world, only they do so in different ways and with different things[319] according to the best of their knowledge. What is common in them is that they did not retire to loneliness to obtain only lower-level Self-expansions,[320] that form of Self-expansion is short-term, and has little effect on other's lives. Instead, they chose to use the good within them for the common good, for all.

That seems to be how 'heaven' works. People who, at the end of their lives, can look back and say that they gave, are the people who can enter a state of endless Self-expansion. Is this foolish? Is Self-expansion being over-emphasized so that it can explain even heaven and hell? The answer, albeit speculative,[321] is: near-death experiences have been studied scientifically in medical procedures, whereby a patient is placed in a state of clinical 'death', then brought back to life. Psychologists interviewed such patients about their near-death experiences. There were two common points in their accounts:

o people relived their lives before the moment of death; and
o they were completely calm, saw lights, heard pleasant voices etc.

By combining the two, assuming that the latter is an extremely Self-expanded condition, the process then works in the following way. We relive those experiences of the highest emotional intensity. Amongst these there will initially be intensely Self-narrowed and intensely Self-expanded experiences.[322] All of these memories, mixed with the actual state, result in those who were mainly Self-narrowed maintaining a Self-narrowed (evil-minded, pessimistic, violent) state; and those who are generally Self-expanded (positive thinking, helpful, giving) will become even more Self-expanded. The import of this moment of death is that it is the last a person will ever have. There is no absolution of this, and no chance for explanation, so that it becomes a constant moment. The key to understanding this lies in the wrong – or at least altered – sense of time: when we relive a whole life (70-80 years, more than 2.2 billion seconds), it is possible that the last second may feel as if it lasts for decades.

Imagine the worst (the most Self-narrowed) moment of your life: great pain, terrible news etc. Fix that mental condition in yourself. Now, imagine that you are in that mental state for 70-80 years. Is that not the greatest punishment you can ever receive? Permanent living purgatory? Is this not Hell that you receive for your sins? Is this not the opposite of what we call Heaven (70 years of constant Self-expansion, similar to a 70 years long orgasm)?

Did God create in us this alteration of the sense of time (when one-tenth of a second feels like 70 years before death)? Or is this only a biological fact everyone has to decide for himself? Which hormones and neurotransmitters could do that

---

[319] people who help others; give knowledge; create beauty or things that make our lives easier
[320] for example, sex, eating, autotelic reading
[321] due to its nature
[322] for example, our first kiss, marriage, childbirth etc., and matters that are sins according to the Ten Commandments: intrigue (gossiping), stealing, cheating, etc.

are not known, but if there is a system like this, is it both a work of God or the result of evolution?

There have been people throughout history who "came back from the dead", so that their remaining lives run down in front of their eyes due to an existential danger. After they related their experiences, the concept of heaven and hell could be established, which closely related to the good in the life of these people.

To properly interpret this chapter...

As the theory described has not yet been verified by experiment, it is not so robust, or usable, in many cases. What can be stated is that the theory may not work in a chemically 'pure' form, but that the combination of these paths is close to an actual answer for somebody. Therefore, real happiness can be attained by those who mix the different paths described, even if one of the aims overtakes the others by some distance. Altruists who do not have children, or who are not interested in aesthetic beauty, will have difficulty in being happy. It does not matter how nice or attractive these things are but, as we are sated and sickened if we eat chocolate all of the time, so permanent stimulation of the region of the brain dealing with cognitive schema will lead to burn-out.

The good news is that, in order to be happy, we need to do no more than find our path, and set out upon it. Finding our path needs self-reflection and higher knowledge about ourselves, but struggling with these questions may be the nicest problem we can ever have.

Finally, a personal intuition on finding an easier path. Whatever that path may be, we have to give something to those around us. You might ask, to whom, and what, should I give? "To whom" are those who are important to us: our children, nation, mankind, or any group one belongs to or that is important in our lives. "What" is whatever you can give that has value; knowledge, health, money, technology, or advice.

Principal points covered in this chapter:
- can happiness be defined
- religious Self-expansion
- death

GLOSSARY

Aha experience:
> an insight that manifests itself suddenly (from German 'Aha-Erlebnis'). Here, 'aha' expresses triumph.

Cognitive schema (plural: schemata):
> basic element of thought; a mental model depicting the environment. Examples include: concepts, shapes, categories, technologies etc.

Deadlock (nadir):
> taken from the world of sport; a situation where a worse position cannot be achieved. Long-distance runners know that, at the start of a race, they will feel increasingly tired until they almost give up as their legs fail. Then, suddenly, something changes, the tiredness disappears, and that is replaced by a feeling of limitless power. After deadlock, athletes feel as if they are able to run without stopping.

Levels:
> cognitive schemata are not only connected to each other, but they are also arranged in a hierarchy (often visualized as a pyramid). Each schema (except the top schema) can have children (lower-level) and parent (higher-level) schemata. The level at which a schema is found indicates the complexity of the phenomenon it models. The top-level schema depicts the whole universe.

Maslow's pyramid:
> the popular name of Maslow's hierarchy of needs. The higher needs in this hierarchy only come into focus when the lower needs in the pyramid are satisfied. According to Maslow, people develop their personalities by rising higher and higher in this hierarchy, until they reach the top level. A similar concept is presented in Chapter 12.

Paradigm:
> a philosophical and theoretical framework of a scientific school or discipline, within which theories, laws, and generalizations, and the experiments performed in support of them, are formulated. Broadly, a philosophical or theoretical framework of any kind. (Taken from the Merriam-Webster Online Dictionary – http://www.merriam-webster.com/dictionary/paradigm)

IMAGES PROTECTED BY COPYRIGHT

illustration nr.	located	license	owner (attribution)	change log
4	http://en.wikipedia.org/wiki/Image:Maslow%27s_hierarchy_of_needs.svg	GFDL*	http://commons.wikimedia.org/wiki/User:J._Finkelstein	deleted 'of ' six times in the row 'Safety'
5	http://commons.wikimedia.org/wiki/Image:God2-Sistine_Chapel.png	Public Domain	http://commons.wikimedia.org/wiki/User:QuartierLatin1968	converted to black and white
10	http://en.wikipedia.org/wiki/Image:CrosswordUK.svg	GFDL*	http://en.wikipedia.org/wiki/User:Michael_J	inserted words; converted to black and white
32	http://upload.wikimedia.org/wikipedia/commons/1/11/Sterappel_dwarsdrsn.jpg	GFDL*	http://commons.wikimedia.org/wiki/User:Rasbak	converted to black and white
34	http://en.wikipedia.org/wiki/Image:C-3PO.jpg	Public Domain	http://en.wikipedia.org/wiki/User:Nricardo	cropped; converted to black and white

*GFDL: GNU Free Documentation License

www.ingramcontent.com/pod-product-compliance
Lightning Source LLC
Chambersburg PA
CBHW071401280526
45787CB00001B/402